ISBN 978-1-333-80469-5
PIBN 10675600

This book is a reproduction of an important historical work. Forgotten Books uses
state-of-the-art technology to digitally reconstruct the work, preserving the original format
whilst repairing imperfections present in the aged copy. In rare cases, an imperfection in
the original, such as a blemish or missing page, may be replicated in our edition. We do,
however, repair the vast majority of imperfections successfully; any imperfections that
remain are intentionally left to preserve the state of such historical works.

1 MONTH OF
FREE
READING

at
www.ForgottenBooks.com

By purchasing this book you are eligible for one month membership to ForgottenBooks.com, giving you unlimited access to our entire collection of over 1,000,000 titles via our web site and mobile apps.

To claim your free month visit:

www.forgottenbooks.com/free675600

English
Français
Deutsche
Italiano
Español
Português

www.forgottenbooks.com

Mythology Photography **Fiction**
Fishing Christianity **Art** Cooking
Essays Buddhism Freemasonry
Medicine **Biology** Music **Ancient
Egypt** Evolution Carpentry Physics
Dance Geology **Mathematics** Fitness
Shakespeare **Folklore** Yoga Marketing
Confidence Immortality Biographies
Poetry **Psychology** Witchcraft
Electronics Chemistry History **Law**
Accounting **Philosophy** Anthropology
Alchemy Drama Quantum Mechanics
Atheism Sexual Health **Ancient History**
Entrepreneurship Languages Sport
Paleontology Needlework Islam
Metaphysics Investment Archaeology
Parenting Statistics Criminology
Motivational

ELEMENTS OF NEGRO RELIGION

BEING A CONTRIBUTION TO THE STUDY OF INDO-BANTU COMPARATIVE RELIGION

BY

W. J. EDMONDSTON-SCOTT

"As Angels in some brighter dreams
  Call to the soul, when man doth sleep;
  So some strange thoughts transcend our wonted themes,
  And into glory peep."

EDINBURGH
EDMONDSTON-SCOTT & CO.
15 FORTH STREET
—
MCMX

Printed by
MORRISON & GIBB LIMITED
Edinburgh

To the Memory of

MY LITTLE BROTHER CHARLIE

FOR HIS
CHRISTIAN EXAMPLE AND FORTITUDE

THE FIRST-FRUITS OF INDO-BANTU COMPARATIVE RELIGION

ARE DEDICATED

CONTENTS

CHAPTER IV

THE WORSHIP OF ANCESTORS

CHAPTER V

ESCAPING DEATH BY MEANS OF DEATH

CHAPTER VI

THE NEGRO'S ASPECTS OF GOD

INTRODUCTION

"Come now, and let us reason together, saith the Lord."

THE object of this work is twofold: first, to present to the reader a brief but concise account of negro religion as it is to-day, and as it was before the Christian era; and secondly, from purely scientific motives to supply the foundation to the study of Indo-Bantu Comparative Religion, on which others may rear their fabrics in security and, perhaps, peace. Thus while the work professes to be simple and unassuming in nature, so guileless, indeed, that even he who runs may read, it claims, nevertheless, to be a scientific study on scientific lines, which, to be thoroughly understood and appreciated, must be read with the scientific vision.

The present work is doubtless unique of its kind, because it deals solely with a single branch of the human race, rather than with "comparative humanity" as most other studies in Comparative Religion tend to do, deserving on that account to be fitly styled, *Family Religion of the Negro*. So intimately is this family religion linked to the civilisation of the negroes that it can scarce be dissociated from their history, whether ancient or

modern, and if once this salient fact be recognised, the general aspect of the negro faith must
necessarily be viewed in different light. With
all the outward semblance of modernness it has
yet the genuine stamp of antiquity, the fundamental elements of the faith being traceable to a
very remote age.

In the following pages are described only
those modern religious beliefs whose history can
be traced back to about 4000 B.C. The reader is
thus enabled, from the evidence laid before him,
to judge for himself the state of negro religion as
it was a short while after the Flood; and if he at
all should give the subject his earnest consideration, he must perforce come to the palpable
conclusion that the modern Bantu negro has
descended in the scale of civilisation, whereas
his remote ancestors lived up to higher ideals
which he, at least, has never attained, and for
which he has showed no aspirations. It will,
moreover, be readily granted that the negro's
belief in the former superiority of his antediluvian forefathers, and his faith in the divinity
of man, entitle him to a share of the world's
esteem, almost in preference to those of our
own age who, presuming to be wise and
learned evolutionists, endeavour to trace the
religious history of humanity back to a stage
of bestial degradation in defiance of the best
traditions of men to the contrary.

Religion is not subject to evolution, because evolution traces the progress of things, whereas religion never progresses, since it emanates from God who is perfection absolute. If we should speak loosely of religion progressing, we have forgotten that religion has only the power to elevate. Evolution, then, cannot be with safety applied to religion. Its laws apply to the physical world exclusively, but have little place or part in spiritual matters. God is not subject to evolution, and God is a Spirit. In lesser degree, men are spiritual, and in their case also evolution cannot be said to have any influence in regard to their spiritual welfare or elevation. By natural sequence, we find that the fundamental principles of religion remain immutable throughout the ages, however surrounded by the change and decay which human progress brings in its train. The negro of 4000 B.C. is thus discovered to have the same faith in God, added to a wide knowledge of His power, wisdom, goodness, and holiness, as the negro of the twentieth century A.D. Whatever may be said, therefore, about the progress and decay of negro civilisation during the last five millenniums, the fact is indisputable that his religion has always been stationary because it could not progress. Its duty is to teach the eternity of life, which it tries to elevate nearer to God, but to teach progress is alien to its spirit and beyond its power. The world may progress, and afterwards discover that its old ideas of progress must die before the coming of the new ; but God's teachings are meant to elevate, and whom God has elevated time nor eternity can deprive of his station of honour and dignity.

On the reasonable assumption that religion is unchangeable and cannot progress, that the faith of the antediluvian negro was very much what it is to-day among his direct descendants, I have taken the liberty to ignore the existence of the many scientists of our day who trace modern beliefs and superstitions to debased ideals of primitive humanity, and kept to the historical side of the subject so as to prove that negro religion about 4000 B.C. was ennobling, because it owed its power and essence largely to divine revelation. Indo-Bantu Comparative Religion is thus seen to have its historical side, because it presents, in a scientific manner, the state of Indo-Bantu Religion as it was in the beginning.

A very natural and proper question may now be asked regarding the use and signification of the term *Indo-Bantu*, and the answer to this leads up to the truly scientific aspect of the subject. It is here that the Science of Indo-Bantu Comparative Philology makes its entrance on the field, its one and only aim being to prove, by means of philological laws applied to the modern negro languages, that about 4000 B.C. or thereby lived a negro race in Bengal—conveniently termed Indo-Bantu—which migrated westwards in course of time to the distant lands of Europe and Africa; and that its immediate representatives of to-day are the Kol negroes of Bengal, the Basques of Europe, and the Bantu negroes of Central and Southern Africa. Together, therefore, the Kol, Basques, and Bantu belong, scientifically speaking, to one family, the direct descendants of the ancient Indo-Bantu race of Bengal. Despite their apparent diversity in language, habits, and customs, they are brothers of the same blood, children of the same stock; and that fact being admitted—it happens to be incontrovertible—it follows as a simple matter of logic that religious beliefs and superstitions held in common by the Kol, Basque, and Bantu negroes are the exclusive property of the Indo-Bantu family, and accordingly a great antiquity can be claimed for them. Once negro beliefs are proved common to the Indo-Bantu race of to-day, they are simultaneously proved to have formed part of the ancient Indo-Bantu religion which flourished in Bengal ages ago, and from which modern negro religion has derived its inspiration and strength. In the present work, therefore, it will be found that the Kol, Basque, and Bantu negroes always loom in the forefront, because its chief aim is to reconstruct the family religion of the negro by a careful comparison and analysis of the fundamental beliefs of the Indo-Bantu family of to-day.

Thus is it that by the exact methods of Indo-Bantu Comparative Religion we are enabled to discover the ancient state of Indo-Bantu Religion, as well as to trace modern negro thought and belief away back to the days before the great Flood in the Indian Archipelago, when the several races of humanity were scattered to every quarter of the globe. In many ways, the negro benefits by the comparison, for he has no need to be ashamed of his past. And although he is to-day our poor relation, being closer knit to us by the ties of blood and language than is the Turk, Hungarian, or Jew, we ought not on account of his abject poverty to regard him in utter contempt, or repudiate an affinity which the laws of science will uphold in the face of civilised opposition.

The negro is denied to have a religion, and it is the purpose of this work to remove that erroneous superstition. For the first time, perhaps, the negro will be allowed to tell his own tale, as far as it can be told, in his own words and after his own methods of argument, and then the reader will be the better able to understand the many causes which give negro religion its enormous vitality. The faith of millions of negroes does not flourish on agnosticism, atheism, or idolatry, but has a character of its own, the reflex of the spiritual life of the people. While found wanting in many respects, it is yet shown to be, fundamentally at least, in no ways hostile to the spirit of Christianity, with which it has much in common, and could easily be levelled up to the standard of Christian ideals if missionaries and others were less ignorant of the value of its teachings as a means to reach the deeper chords of the negro's nature, which vibrate to the native religion alone. And despite the supercilious attitude affected, especially in America, towards the unoffending negro, with a riper knowledge of his spiritual life will come the fascination of Negro Religion. If we are better than the negro, we owe it to the higher ideals of Christianity, not to ourselves. But at the same time let us remember the negro is no more a degraded heathen savage than the average white man. Do you think your threepenny bit is better than your half-crown because it goes more regular to church? You will find that the negro, too, has his tale of divine revelation to tell. He has a message for the world, and through his advocates of peace awaits to make it known. The negro is the hope of Africa. His message of revelation deserves a sympathetic hearing.

If negro religion be negatived by a callous world, it is done surely from unintentional ignorance. Negro religion has but to be viewed in different perspective before its real worth can be ascertained. And supposing the popular but old-fashioned, preconceived ideas about the negro receive a rude and sudden shock by being upset, the change of view will be found beneficial. You will see the old made new, the prosaic and un-interesting become stranger than fiction. Negro religion is essentially novel, and novelty is the very breath of romance. It has, moreover, the ring of inspired truth, and the character which lends it the charm of originality.

In the meanwhile, the negro may be left to speak for himself, and confess the native faith which divine revelation has inspired. A careful perusal of the *Elements* will testify to the negro's sincerity of belief, besides disclose to advantage the inner workings of his active mind, and the vital principles which confirm him in his faith. And I doubt not, if the objects of this work are attained, it will succeed in raising the negro in the public esteem. The author is an advocate who pleads his case for the negro without fear of reproach. The author is a soldier who has crossed the Rubicon, and summons his legions of right-thinking men and women to battle with the anti-negro hosts of ignorance and prejudice, and the world's un-Christian attitude of indif-ference towards the spiritual elevation of the shepherdless millions of Darkest Africa.

ELEMENTS OF NEGRO RELIGION

———◆———

CHAPTER I

NEGRO STORIES OF THE CREATION

"Life is real! Life is earnest!
And the grave is not its goal;
'Dust thou art, to dust returnest'
Was not spoken of the soul."

Religion as a Science.—Religion is the Science of Life. It teaches eternity. Brief may be the portion of the world's spectral eurekas, but amongst them all, Life stands unmoved, eternal and unchangeable as the Universe which hides its origin in silence mysterious. On all sides surrounded by change and decay, it never forsakes hope, even amidst the ashes of the dead. Nay rather, it has the restless and indomitable spirit of genius to wage unceasing warfare with death in all its protean forms, eternally weaving anew the strands which death had tried to break. Life is spirit which death cannot alter or destroy, because

God is a **S**pirit, and God is Life, whom death, indeed, never dared to approach with its defiling touch.

Thus regarded, religion becomes the science which teaches men how to live and reason, and to learn of God, the Creator of life. Its genius and strength are derived from the Giver of life, and having exercised the minds of men from the beginning must continue so to do till Time has ceased to be. Measureless and infinite, it abides not the restrictions of time and space; is immutable as its Creator; and supernatural, because it appeals solely to the living but immaterial nature in man, which never suffers the pains of physical decay, nor knows the bitter taste of the death-cup. If God's message to the world, that death is but the door to eternal life, have the ring of truth, where is death's sting? It is not death to die. To die is gain.

Religion is not, as some choose to think, a superstition engendered first in savage bosoms. It knows no difference in degrees, because God is no respecter of persons; and matures in every clime and country,—wherever, in fact, the human race has come to dwell. Nor is it a mere supernatural fungus extracting a sickly nurture from human fear and fancy. It draws its essence from an outside force, of which it is the medium of expression as well as its interpreter; and while it lives by the sustaining power derived from that force, its growth can be quickened or retarded, according as the individual desires, or refuses, to live and work in harmony with the still, small element expanding outward from within.

Religion and Character.—It is a true saying of the poet, "An honest man's the noblest work of God." Nobility of character, controlled and guided by the sustaining influence of religion, is beyond the power of the world to make. True character expresses individuality—call it eccentricity if you will—and carries with it the genuine stamp of a noble mind which lives above the trite and commonplace the world calls fashionable. True character is the divine essence in a man, the outward assertion of the "I AM" in human guise. As a contrast, the world tends to reduce society to a uniform level, an uninteresting and prosaic sameness; and in this follows out the best traditions of the Devil, who, loving the darkness, is essentially a shady character. He was a rank socialist from the beginning of time, and a leveller of good character, because it reminded him too much of the suzerainty of God, and the power of good over evil. Now, where religion is a living force, where the spiritual life is real and earnest, true character must develop, being part of the spiritual wealth whose growth is fostered by its means. To rise above the sordid aims and grovelling ambitions of a selfish humanity a man *must* have character his own, and individuality which the world will surely ridicule as a type of madness or eccentricity, even while it be deeply jealous that character should display a silent-moving power at work, such as moves the lower minds to feelings of bitterest enmity and scorn.

Religion cannot progress. — Compared with human ideas of wisdom or knowledge, religion seems elusive and irrational, especially to those who know little or nothing about it. Starting from general statements and facts very difficult to establish in a logical way, it proceeds to teach a knowledge of God, and His relationship to man ; but as its every lesson refers to another world from ours and to the invisible essence in our physical natures, the reason of its elusiveness is not difficult to understand.   This is yet a virtue rather than otherwise.   The elusiveness of religion is but inchoate revelation, and hence its unrevealed truths can scarce be impugned by questions of mere logic which time can answer whensoever it will.   And should the frailty of human intellect cause them to be altered to suit the fashions of the hour, the change from the immutable to the transient leads straight to confusion and error.   Fundamental truths about God and the Unseen cannot be tested by weak moral senses, nor subjected to change with impunity.   Religion cannot change, because it cannot progress.   As it starts from perfection absolute, change must necessarily subject it to devolution, and possibly decay.

Religion takes many forms when influenced by race and environment; yet everywhere there is a radical sameness apparent in all its varied forms, despite the load of improved ideas with which the several races of mankind have burdened their original faith.   To these "Addenda to Religion," acceptable to one race but seldom another, are to be traced those vagaries which tend to confine a particular type of faith within certain prescribed bounds.   Superficially considered, religion then becomes a matter of geographical position.   The Buddhist, Hindu, Mahometan, Confucianist, and Christian, have each a limited sphere of influence, outside which they one and all breed racial and religious discord.   It is certain, nevertheless, that the leading tenets of the various sects are fundamentally alike, because they convey the same spiritual messages to men; and, accordingly, the inexplicable lack of harmony amongst them is not due to faults inherent in the original faith, but to the proportion and superabundance of local ideas, rites, and customs, which are the real factors in determining the local form and colouring of any faith.   God gives us inspiration when He will, but our religion is as we make it. True religion, unaltered by human error, untransformed by the accretions of superstition, is incapable of localisation, and never at war with itself.

Negro Faith.—The faith of the Bantu negro has for its foundation the primary belief in a benign Creator who reigns supreme in the universe. God is not immanent. He is a personal Creator, and a person cannot be immanent. He is Mind Supreme, and immanent as thought is immanent. God is Thought. By prayer we gain His ear, because prayer is thought, the soul's sincere desire, and thought is the first faculty of the soul, the telepathic instinct of the spirit. Nor can it truthfully be said that the modern negro's conception of God has evolved in his mind through course of time, or by some strange unfathomable process of reasoning. The belief has descended to him from antediluvian ancestors,—and, in a purely historical sense, from the Kol negroes of Bengal, who are the fathers of the Bantu of Africa. Irrespective of caste or culture, it appeals to him by virtue of its simplicity, and besides, satisfies his inner being instinctive, he knows not how or why, with a yearning for a better and happier life. He has not yet attained those heights of unbelief and indifference, when it is held proper to question or deny facts beyond one's mental grasp with the learned saw, "We do not know." His first care is to despise a difficulty by beating round it, and so to begin with, he takes for granted the truth of three great postulates—

> God the Uncreated Creator.
> God the Beginning.
> God the End.

Such is the foundation on which securely rests the mighty fabric of negro religion. It excludes superstition altogether, and as the negro can readily distinguish between these two classes of belief, inasmuch as his faith in God is a thing apart from his personal ideas and observations, theological bickerings are limited to differences of opinion about the meaning and importance of local rites and customs. The absence of sectarian rivalry and jealousy is explained by the recognised barrier between religion with its open simplicity, and superstition with its ceremony and forms of ritual. The one is above the world of wrangling, the precursor of God with the message of peace and goodwill to men. The other is over-productive of quarrels, persecution, and petty tyranny, because the human element is allowed to predominate.

The Fear of God.—What is writ large over negro religion is the fear of God, a fear which asserts its influence most in that domain of thought where man's relation to Nature and Nature's God finds utterance. Nature is not God, and cannot arrogate to itself the attributes of God, since it is not a spirit. Having no spiritual power of itself, it can transmit none to the material world. To the average negro, it appears but the shadowiest image of God, and its moods the working of His emotions. God is a Spirit; Nature is not, and yet through it the spirit of God sometimes manifests itself to men, the negro conception of His personality being similar to that so admirably expressed by the poet—

> "He plants His footsteps in the sea,
> And rides upon the storm."

In this way, the thunder is believed to be His angry voice; the whirlwind His æry chariot; the earthquake the noise of His footsteps; and the lightning His sword wherewith He smites the people who have sinned.

Fear, however, is not the offspring of love, and if, nowadays, undue stress is laid on the fear of God, it is because the blighting influence of Spiritualism has partly burned out the old native love toward God in the all-consuming flames of human dread of spirit-beings. It is unjust to say that the chief end of negro religion is to avert divine wrath and its consequences; that it is a crude art to pacify the angry spirits of ancestors; a form of devil-worship showing superstition and idolatry at their lowest and worst. God is not always angry with the children He knows to be frail; and so, deep hidden beneath the surface of ignorance and fear, is to be sought the genuine faith, whose creed is love and mercy.

Revealed and Natural Religion.—The negro is not a worshipper of Nature or the mysterious. The blue Nyanza with its cool depths and strange denizens, the dark pool with its snaky occupants, the forest-glade alive with the hum of bird and insect, and ever and anon with the rustle of the snake and the roar of the lion, have all a fascination to move his fancy, but equally fail to stir his religious feelings. Face to face with the mystical and unknown, his ignorance begets fear and superstition, but he will bow the knee to none of them. He has not learned to people the seas and rivers with nymphs, nor the woods with sylvan dryads and satyrs. However much impressed by Nature's grandeur and mystery, his mind turns instinctively to the Power he believes is acting through it. Never did he obtain that knowledge of God from the mere study of Nature, for, granted that the negro is an observant and practical thinker, he is transparent and shallow at the best. His exposition of Nature is very simple, and agrees with that of his forefathers who taught him. Nature supplies the talent which imitates and reflects, but behind the talent is the moving genius, which is God.

Negro religion thus makes room for two distinct systems of belief, one of which is sub-

sidiary to the other.   The gulf between the two
is the difference that separates Revealed from
Natural Religion, and under one or other of these
all beliefs are to be classified, according as they
express in negro parlance—

Man's relation and duty to God.
Man's relation and duty to Nature.

When taxed about his personal beliefs, the
negro becomes unusually reticent ; and for this
respectful attitude towards matters spiritual he
has been roundly abused and condemned by
European traders and travellers alike, as an infidel
and savage without a knowledge of God.   And yet,
Comparative Philology proves convincingly that
the negroes have known God and understood His
attributes for over five thousand years.   Too
often the wanderers from Europe, after abusing
Africa's welcome hospitality, returned to denounce
the negroes with undue harshness and pre-
cipitancy, led astray, in most cases, by native
spiritualism, and reluctant to search for the truth
beneath the surface of negro reticence and
apparent atheism.   While they deny the negro's
knowledge of God, they are usually found to
include the native names for " God " in the
vocabularies and grammars they compile.   Such
stories of theirs as should have been told to the
marines may, with good reason, be set aside as
untrustworthy evidence, but, should their truth

be proven by the comparative method as applied to the study of religion, they deserve consideration.

The Negro's attitude to Nature.—Apart from this reticence in confessing God before men, the negro is open and unreserved; in short, regards himself as all-knowing, and certainly is an authority on whatever he knows nothing about. He holds many quaint and curious ideas about natural phenomena, such indeed as have suggested to the learned, or rather the ignorant, what purports to be the beginnings of mythology, but which, to those with experience, have only proved the fertility of the negro's imagination, and his love of the mysterious and occult. The flow and ebb of the tides—metaphorically connected with life and death; the changing seasons, named by some tribes "the green points of grass, the friendly season, the eating season, the reaping season"; and the months with poetic names like "Widow month, Lighting of fires, Swelling grain, Withering pumpkins, Emerald cuckoos, Month of great dust-storms,"—all bear witness to the native's lively fancy, and his close observation of Nature in its varying moods and aspects.

To a more limited extent he is interested in the motions and changes of the planets. The stars, the Pleiades, Jupiter, Venus, the sun and moon, were included in negro astronomy from the earliest times, but further research in this field

was effectually arrested by superstitious ignorance. On this account, it had its penalties as
well as pleasures, and, like the cultivation of
plants and flowers, star-gazing was discouraged
owing to its evil associations with witchcraft.

The Value of Fossil Idiom.—Old negro
beliefs and traditions are often found enshrined
in picturesque idiom. "The sun is going down
to its mother," is the Zulu periphrasis for "sunset," and the Manganja explain this to mean in
their legends that the sun sails home to its
mother in Land Underwaves, nightly coursing
over the celestial waters below the earth. Then
it comes up again on the other side, and speeds
through the upper sky, whose radiant waters
glow with the tropical phosphorescence of starry
myriads. "Good-bye, big golden ball!" cry the
Zulu children, as they think they hear the sun
fall hissing into the sea at night. When it
touches the horizon, it is said to be "hanging";
when there is a solar eclipse, it is playing hide-
and-seek in the bush; and a peculiar idiom for
sunset—which has only an historical significance
—renders it, "The sun has been eaten up by
the pigmies,"—the belief being that the sun sets
in the Land of the African Pigmies, who capture
it with a net and make a good meal of it.

The Light of the Dead.—There is little
or no dawn in the tropics, and as sunrise is
heralded by the shrill cry of strutting chanticleer,

the cocks are said to be "splitting the day."
Like Saturn of old, they cleave day and night
apart.   The sun's return from the winter-solstice
is its "return to fetch out the ploughmen"; and
from the summer-solstice, its "return to fetch the
bird-watchers" to look after the ripening corn-
fields.   To be wise is to have "daylight" in the
mind; to be ignorant is to be "benighted."
Hence, to say that there is "night" in a certain
kraal means, in Zulu, a paradise of fools.   Lastly,
when the sea has ebbed its full, the Zulus say
that it is "dead"—*ulwandhle luvile*—for with
the ebbing tide the souls of deceased warriors
depart for the Happy Mansions.

The moon is less beloved of the negro than
star or sun or sea.   To him it is the ever-present
emblem of Time and Death, and as such appears
in native tales; the root *anga*, "moon," with its
baneful associations, being fittingly illustrated by
its analogy in Basque—*ill-argi*, "moon"—literally, the "light of the dead."

The moon's influence on men is pernicious.
The wicked planet bears them malice, and the
unhappy mortal who is "bemooned" at the
bewitching time of night, acts and thinks differently than when in sober sense.   Perhaps he
loses his right mind entirely, and then he thinks
and jokes, in a sublunary manner, without per-
ceiving how his neighbours call him "moon-
struck," a lunatic who is always talking "moon-

shine." In a less lighter vein, the negroes fear the moon as a murderess. Many, in fact, believe that death came from that quarter, or at least by the moon's agency, and liken it to an ugly old cannibal or witch, who loves to devour the people she calls her insects. And it was because she herself was subject to decay and death that she transmitted these evils to men.

From the earliest ages, time was reckoned by the phases of the moon, and as once a month the planet disappeared from view, men observed that it grew old and died like themselves. Of what the wandering celestial is made, nobody can tell, and why it waxes and wanes passes negro calculation. But this is known for a certainty : the moon lives for a few weeks, wastes away with age and dies, never to return. It fades into nothingness, and is replaced by an entirely new creation—the New Moon.

The death of the old moon is sincerely mourned by the Zulus and neighbouring tribes, the period of total darkness before the day of the New Moon being spent in rigorous fasting. These are the "dark days" on which the Zulus do no work, but sit in their huts eating medicine, until the "white days" of the New Moon come round. Similarly, a lunar eclipse is a public calamity, because, through celestial witchcraft, the moon might be killed. To frighten away the invisible cause of witchcraft, the natives set up loud cries and wails, sufficient to disturb the soundest slumbers of Nature.   For conscience' sake, the negroes make a joyless noise, and for peace' sake, lions take to the mountains, and crocodiles seek the deepest holes in the rivers. Far different are the rejoicings made on the day of New Moon.   Its arrival is ushered in with much festivity, and as the natives make merry they offer thanks to God for recreating their favourite luminary.   Thus, say the negroes, change and decay brought death, and death brought life.

The Personality of Nature.—In common with the sun and moon, the sky is allotted a certain amount of vital consciousness.   It has a *persona* more masculine than the moon, and is usually addressed as "he."   When it hails or rains, the Bengal negro exclaims, *areljadae, gamajadae !* "he hails, he rains!" and this idiomatic type of expression is also applicable to the thunder and lightning.   Its occurrence in the Basque and Zulu tongues offers convincing evidence that ages ago the negroes treated such natural phenomena in quite a personal way, because a religious meaning was attached.   The rain, hail, snow, thunder and lightning, were nothing in themselves.   Rather their importance lay in a deeper sense, as they were the agents which expressed visibly to men the will and moods of a greater force acting through them.

It is this rooted belief that has so long actuated the negroes, and brought them to think of Nature as a personal force, even although they have refused to worship or deify any of the elements.

Nature Folklore.—When a fierce storm bursts forth, the people say, *i-zulu*, the sky, is angry, and is "stamping" or roaring along the countryside. Especially are the signs of his wrath seen when a tree, house, animal, or man is struck by lightning; and as *i-zulu* is seldom dissociated from the rains and tropical cloud-bursts that he brings with him, up-country he sometimes bears the same name as the rain. Of *i-zulu's* habits and ways, legend has many a tale to tell. A Yao story describes how once the lightning flashed and killed a man, and then ran back to heaven. The people complained of its wickedness. *I-zulu* was very sorry, and sent down the rain to let the people make beer for the mourning.

In another legend, the rainbow is called God's bow, and the lightning His arrow for killing meat. Once upon a time God drew His bow and shot four stars. He picked them up, boiled them in His cooking-pot, and ate them. The stars had the flavour of finely cooked flesh, and were as sweet as honey to the taste. Shortly after, an arrogant chief asked a loan of the wonderful bow, and ventured to draw it.

But, alas for human frailty! Like Phæthon, he paid for his temerity with his life, making God so vexed at the untoward accident that He went away from the abodes of men. Nobody could tell whither He had gone, but He vanished from earth to return no more, leaving behind the rainbow, which He set in the sky to remind His people of His former sojourn among them here below.

It is passing strange that in the several negro terms for "rainbow," an old name for its divine owner should also have survived. The Yao call it *ukunju wa Mulungu*, "the Almighty's bow," but the Manganja have preserved the far more ancient phrase, *uta wa Lesa*, "the bow of Lesa," who is reckoned the same as *Mulungu*—the *Unkulunkulu* of the Zulus. The equivalent in Santali is *Lita ak'*, "the bow of Lita," but as the Santals have forgotten all about Lita, it is uncertain what the name of *Lita* signified about 4000 B.C. Suffice it to say that Santali *Lita* and Bantu *Lesa* are one and the same, and as both correspond to the Etruscan deity *Leinth*, the Lord of the Rainbow, the negro's earliest conception of *Lita* was evidently that of Jehovah with the rainbow-halo round His head.

Influence of Literature and Art.—A stage of thought further removed from the negro was attained by the Etruscan and Pelasgian negroes, encouraged doubtless by the progress of Literature and Art. The thunder, lightning, rain, and snow were pictured as gods, and ceased to be merely natural agents. But poetical as were the artists' ideas, the meaning of their names was never forgotten. Vulcan remained the "Lightning-flash," Phaola the "Rain," and Thurms the "Thunder." Above them all stood out the figure of Hermes, a deity much in favour with an agricultural race. He was the *Thurms* of Etruria, and the *Tiurm* of the Basques, the meaning of his name being made obvious from Basque *tiurm*, "thunder," and Zulu *dūma*, "thunder" (= *durma*). Thurms, the servant and messenger of God, was a luck - bringer like Hermes, because he was the "Thunderer." For as thunder in the tropics is the sure sign of fruitful showers, it has become a welcome sound —the harbinger of good fortune; and it is this negro idea which pervades the character of the several Thunderers of the ancients.

Other elements were personified, like *Ankelos*, the "Dawn," the rosy-fingered messenger of morn, and *Charun*, "Time," — pictured on Etruscan ware as a terrible god, armed with hammer and sword instead of the usual sickle and crossbones. In addition, there was the evil spirit of "Fire," *Ushil*, who is recognised in Central Africa as *Chiuta*; *Vulcan*, and *Sethlans*, the smith who forges the thunderbolts. So in a tale from the French Congo, it is also a clever blacksmith who makes the lightning and thunder, and has his forge set deep in the heart of a gloomy forest.

Among minor deities, the Etruscan goddess *Kupra* can scarce be omitted. She was the *Cybele* of Greece and Phrygia, and is to-day the *Kubulwana* of the Zulus, by whom she is regarded as the goddess of rain and corn, having her home above *i-zulu*, the sky. Once every year her festival is held at the hoeing of the *amabele* corn, and as women are the leading farm-labourers it is observed chiefly by them. Great licence prevails at the festival, and even children play no insignificant part. Girls masquerade in boys' clothes, and go about from door to door like guisers, begging for corn to make beer. Their modest request is rarely refused, as to do so amid the general plenty is to admit poverty or miserliness. The celebration of Cybele's Feast is thus a time of public rejoicing and thanksgiving, and is equally familiar to the children of Europe as to the negroes of Bengal and Zululand.

The sun sank beneath the sea, and the Pelasgians, believing that the latter supported the world, deified it as *Atlas*. They could not forget, however, that Atlas and the sea were synonymous terms. By parity of reasoning, they personified many elements like the winds, or objects like mountains, rivers, and lakes. It was a kind of Natural Religion, but they knew full

well what they did, since they understood the
meaning of the terms they used. With the
Romans and Greeks, who adopted the old names
they never understood, it was otherwise. To
them it was Religion without morality, Mythology without significance ; and by imitating the
ancient personifying and artistic habit to excess,
they reduced primitive religion to absurdity by
deifying anything they chose. Even abstract
terms, like Peace and War, Concord and Discord, came to be worthy of national reverence ;
but such a worship marked human progress with
religious decadence. It was too apt to mistake
the pomp of ritual for faith ; and so the ritual
of religion prospered as the other faded into
insignificance, till poets asked why their ministers
of religion did not laugh when they met each
other on the streets of Rome.

Among the Etruscans, Natural Religion was
never the true faith. God was not Nature but
Thini, "Creator"—the *um-Dali* of the Zulus ;
and the corresponding female element was
Thalna or Juno. He lived far away above the
sky, and had a regular order of priests to attend
to His private and public worship. The many
titles He bore included such as *Thini*, "Creator,"
Aemi, "Father," *Leinth*, "Rainbow-Lord," besides the general name of *Aesar*, "God"—the
Ashur of the Canaanites and *Isor* of the Santals.
To Libyan negroes, *Thini* was *um-Dali*, or *Zeus*

Ammon, and Strabo briefly sums up Libyan faith, when he says of the Africans that they regarded Ammon as the Creator, immortal, and the Cause of all things. Of the existence of other gods and goddesses he was unaware, and his silence is testimony to the monotheism which prevailed among the ancient Libyan Bantu, as well as their freedom from idolatry.

If, therefore, the subject of Natural Religion be considered as a whole, it will be found that it has ever been a secondary factor among mankind, because it is not primitive. It springs up with civilisation wherever Poetry and Art flourish; but is unknown to "Savage Man." The negro has conceived God as Ammon, Mulungu, or Lesa, but He is a personal Creator outside the blind forces of Nature. He stands at the head of a personal religion, and consequently the negro's conception and knowledge of Him must have come through Divine revelation. As he has learned nothing from the study of Nature, it is clear that man's first tutor was God.

Legends of the Creation. — Folktale literature reaches its culminating point among the Kol and Bantu negroes, and this is probably the sole form of oral literature with which antediluvian man was familiar. Centuries before the Flood, tales were sung and stories repeated of the Creation of man; his first experiences and sensations on earth; his Fall, and subsequent punishment.   Further, as they convey the earliest messages of the Word of God, teaching a lofty code of morals with which the modern negro has lost touch, they would, on that score, deserve to be called the oldest religious parables which the world has ever known.   Folktales, in their purest and simplest state, are the surviving relics of an antediluvian literature which has vanished from its ancient abodes, and which will live so long as religion remains to animate them.

The primary class of negro legends deals with the Creation of man, but except that they can be traced historically up to about 4000 B.C., little can be proved regarding their much older origin, and their value as historical evidence. That they contain facts of antediluvian history is beyond question.   Most of the negro nations of India and Africa know something of the days before the Flood, but it is no easy task to dissociate history from a mass of fable, and fable from revealed religion.   The greatest folklorist of antiquity was Æsop the slave, but even this Bantu negro, who charmed and delighted the classic world with his *Fables*, tried only in a small way to condense the ancient wealth of the Bantu moral class of folktales.   From them he drew his inspiration, and amply illustrated the maxims and moral precepts they were intended to convey.

The Yaos of East Africa have a very simple story of the Creation.   God made the sun, moon, and stars; then the earth, which He supplied with trees and flowers, rivers, lakes and mountains; then the beasts; and last of all, Man. Now the sun began to wax proud and fierce, and said in his heart, "I will shine fiercely and destroy the sons of God." The ill-effects became first apparent when men grew very black, and God seeing this, sent down the rain to slake their raging thirst and burning heat. After a while, men died and left their friends. They became "gods" and said, "Come, let us send rain to our people." Their pleadings with the Creator succeeded, and ever since the first man died, the spirits of ancestors have been venerated as saints. Whenever drought comes on the land, they are asked to persuade Mulungu to open the bottles of heaven, and let out the imprisoned showers.

Animal Lore and its Lessons.—In many tales of this kind, animals figure largely, doubtless because the native knowledge about them is extensive. They are preferred before men in the order of Creation, but this may be explained by the fact that the natives found wild animals whithersoever they turned. Long experience and familiarity have accustomed the negro to the ways of beasts, birds, reptiles, and insects, and in no class of literature is his knowledge displayed to greater advantage than in the folktales.

Among the animals, the lion is an easy first. He is a by-word for strength and boldness, but is easily outwitted by the cunning of weaker creatures. The moral to be drawn from the king of the forest is that brute force reigns supreme in the physical world, which may be overcome and outdone by craft. Mind surpasses brute force, and by parity of reasoning—

> "The good old rule, the simple plan,
>   That they should take who have the power,
>   And they should keep who can,"

is not to be taken in its literal sense, because the negro moral applies equally to men as to brutes.

The serpent, naturally enough, is cunning and vindictiveness combined, nursing his wrath long after his victim be dead and gone. The monkey is a vivacious youth, ready to fool and cheat anybody, and as slippery as an eel when driven into a tight corner. The rabbit excels Reynard in astuteness and legerdemain, while the elephant is a solemn, easy-going old judge, often fooled and brow-beaten by his long-necked advocate, the antelope. In an age before man was created, all these animals could speak, but their constant chatter, chatter, chatter so annoyed Mulungu that he struck them all dumb. Since that age, the brute creation has maintained a golden silence, content to listen quietly to the music of the spheres, and spend its days in silent rumination.

A few animals are bound up with fetishism and witchcraft, and so are tabu to good people. For instance, the baboon and hyena are the creatures on whose backs the wizards ride through the air. Should one have the misfortune to meet them, he dare not look behind for fear he be hurled away through the air by unseen hands. Now, they have become omens of ill-luck, and the untoward sight of either is enough to send the traveller home, or make the labourer stop work till he has eaten medicine.

The cat is another animal of ill omen. It is known by the company it keeps. It would be easier to find the sea without salt than a witch without her feline servant, and for this reason the cat is quite able to bewitch anyone unless he has a care in his approaches. In Zululand, the wicked *i-mpaka* follows anything but the paths of virtue. When it foregathers with a neighbour or two in the kraal at night, the voice of song and saturnalia is heard in the land, and history is made in the small hours of the morning. What rustic poet was it who thus described the historic occasion of a feline meeting :

> " There came a tyrant, and with holy glee
> Thou fought'st against him " ?

Or who the bard who fiercely exclaimed in a burst of poetic frenzy when he awoke to the sounds of revelry by night :

"Two voices are there ; each a mighty voice,
They were thy chosen music, Liberty"?

With sentiments as these the average negro would agree. He holds the cat in pet aversion, but unlike his Bengal forefathers has few scruples about killing it when necessary. Once it is dead, the sound of its voice is stilled, and the touch of the vanished hand less conspicuous in the house. But in Burmah and Bengal, people would shun to kill a cat even to rid themselves of a witch's favourite. They know the cat is exceeding sinful, and the foolhardy man who killed it would have the intolerable burden of its sins exchanged to his shoulders.

Most legends that claim historical pretensions refer the creation of animals to a time long anterior to the advent of man. In the beginning, runs a Yao legend, there lived only Mulungu and the beasts. One day the chameleon went out to fish—for he was a great fisher and trapper— and was agreeably surprised to discover two new species of animals or fish in his net. He was at a loss what to make of them, and fearing to poison himself by eating he wot not of, took them out of his net and let them go. It proved to be a man and woman, and the first thing they did when at liberty was to fire the bush, and make things hot for the chameleon. Up he climbed a tree as fast as his legs would carry him, and so got out of the way ; while Mulungu was grieved at such unworthy conduct, and returned to heaven, saying that He could not live on earth amidst human depravity. However, before He went, He left his last command with them that the spirits of men should ascend on high to Him after they departed their wicked bodies.

The story, with many local differences, is told all over the Bantu area, and is typical of the class of negro folktales whereby the lessons regarding the days of early man are inculcated into the minds of young and old. Those which deal with the Creation appoint him his proper place among the animals, and explain how he was the last of God's creations. They speak quite naturally of the ancient time when God first lived with him on earth, and emphasise how man developed a strange perverseness of character and depravity of nature. As a result, God was compelled, but of His own free will, to return to heaven and live no more on earth, the friend and daily companion of His latest creation.

Historical Legends of the Flood.—The Santals of Bengal have also many traditions regarding their early history; and, being the forefathers of the Bantu, their legends about the origin of man deserve fuller consideration. Unfortunately, few of these can be understood on account of their antiquity, and in many cases the ancient names cannot be traced or explained. *Lita*, the Lord of the Rainbow, has been long since forgotten except in tradition, and the same holds true regarding *Chae, Champa,* and *Mando Sing,* all of whom lived before the Flood in the Indian Archipelago ere they fled into Bengal. Similarly, little is known of *Guja* and *Kara,* two antediluvian brothers, except a few scattered references to them in tradition.

The story of the Deluge is frequently alluded to in folktale; but to discuss Kol and Bantu legends about volcanic eruptions and the floods which followed, or the numberless stories of cities and peoples overwhelmed by the Indian Ocean, is more a matter of history than religion. However mystical or spiritual a meaning such popular stories like to assume, they have an historical value alone. Here it is but right to observe that the negroes of Bengal have not forgotten their ancestors' tales of the Flood, nor those seismic upheavals which forced the negro race of India to emigrate to Bengal from the "Happy Valley," now sunk beneath the waves of the Indian Ocean.

Once upon a time, runs a legend, a flood of fire and rain enveloped every living thing except a brother and sister, who were both blind. During the eruption the two escaped into a mountain cave, the mouth of which they blocked with a huge stone. When the burning lava or "Fire-Water" (*sengel-dah*) flowed down the mountain-side, the stream of fire was diverted from the cave by the great stone block. Thus were the occupants saved. But a different Santal tradition says that the couple lived in a stone house with a stone door, and that, although the flood raged for seven days and nights continuously, it could not beat down the house and overwhelm the brother and sister.

Other local stories affirm that this brother and sister were the first human pair, and the last of *Singbonga's* creations. According to the Kol system, the order of creation was the making of the earth, its vegetation, the domestic animals, the wild beasts, and lastly, the creation of *Pilchu Hadam* and his sister, who ultimately became his wife. The Munda version also supports the tradition that the first man and woman were brother and sister, begotten alike of God. They were bone of His bone and flesh of His flesh, before sin changed their nature and brought death into the world. They were placed in a beautiful valley where they indulged in the simple life. But they knew not how to beget children, till Jehovah (*Singbonga*) taught them, among other arts, how to brew rice-beer. Then they both got drunk, and while under the influence of strong drink, made alliance. From their union sprang the progenitors of the several families into which mankind is grouped.

The amours of the gods and heroes were not unknown to the non-Jewish negroes of Canaan.

The Old Testament proves that the early Canaanites were not without these strange negro legends.
The Canaanite tribes of the Moabites and Ammonites both traced their pedigree to an incestuous
pair.   As a passage in Genesis (chap. xix.)
explains: Lot's two daughters once made him
drunk and then lay with him in succession.   The
first bore a son called Moab, the father of the
Moabites, and the second bore Ben-Ammi, the
father of the children of Ammon.   Such was
one type of folktale current among the negro
Ammonites and others.   Taken in conjunct with
the primitive tales of Bengal they show that, in
the first stages of human history, drunkenness and
incest prevailed, and that, at least in the eyes of
our first parents, neither were held to be vices.

The Creation of Adam and Eve.—A very
peculiar story from Bengal asserts that a goose
and gander (*hãs*, *hãsin*) begat the human race
from their eggs.   Such a legend is too degrading
to be primitive; neither can it be genuine, since
the names of the birds are of Hindu origin.   The
older legends circle round the person of *Pilchu
Hadam*—"Little Man"—sometimes called *Kakar*,
the Speaker.   His sister was *Malin*, "the Be-
witcher," but after she bore him children he
changed her name to *Eva* or *Eve*, because she was
pre-eminently the " Mother."   Indo-Bantu legend
upholds, therefore, the biblical tradition that two
antediluvian persons named *Hadam* and *Eve*,

"man" and "mother," were negroes, and the first parents and begetters of the human family.

The *Hadam* or *Adam* of Canaanite story and legend early made his way into Jewish literature. But he was not wholly understood. He lived to nine hundred and thirty years, because that was the period which the native story-teller believed to separate the first man from his own day. It has to be remembered, moreover, that *Adam* is not a name, but a generic term for "mankind" —equating with Santali *Hadam*. It can thus include women also. God created *Adam*— "mankind." "Male and female created he them, and called their name *Adam* in the day when they were created." The whole legend is clearly an old negro folktale, and not meant to have an historical importance so much as legendary interest. Compared with Kol and Bantu traditions, it bears too many close resemblances to support the belief in its Jewish origin and inspiration. And these may be summarised in a paragraph.

Adam is a generic term for "mankind," and as old as the human race. He is the last of God's creations, and is placed by Him, along with his sister, in the "Happy Valley," or "Garden of Eden." In his time God walks on the earth, and holds communion with him, teaching him a language in which to clothe his thoughts, and how to make use of the objects

around him.   His Fall is caused by the woman,
whose sin is disobedience towards God rather
than moral sin against man.   Nevertheless, she
involves man in her guilt, and drags him down
with her; and subsequently God leaves the
earth because of the increasing wickedness of
the human race.   All these incidents, most of
which are recorded in Sacred Writ, are much
more familiar to the negro nations.   Their
ubiquity in Bengal and Bantu Africa, besides
their general uniformity, prove together that,
since 4000 B.C., the class of tales to which they
belong has spread westwards from Bengal to
Canaan, and from thence to Europe and Africa.

The Divinity of Man.—Among the Bantu,
Adam has many legends to his name.   One
story goes that when God created the first man
and woman from clay, He made them so alike
that He could not tell the one from the other.
The latter smiled at His perplexity, and God
then recognised the woman by the softness of
her smile.   The Kavirondo of the East African
Protectorate trace their descent to a man who
came down from heaven—and this is the usual
prelude to a Bantu genealogy—and landed on
Lamogi Hill, away to the north of Uganda.
There he settled down and married a wife, by
whom he had two sons and four daughters.   To
the names of his children are ascribed those of
the tribes who can claim descent from them.

A Yao legend says that, when God created man, He had to supply him with food to sustain life; then He gave him a lump of iron-ore to occupy his time and tax his ingenuity. Another story speaks of the first human pair as stepping out of a very soft stone, locally termed *kapilim-tiya*; but this seems an echo of the mountain-cave legend, like that of the Santals, rather than a true generic folktale, for it has otherwise no sense.

From the Congo comes a story to the effect that the first man came from heaven. Away above the clouds he used to roam in the happy hunting-grounds; but one day he came to a rift, and looking through saw the earth beneath. He told his wife of the discovery, but as she had opinions of her own she could not be persuaded to go down. The husband went alone, and descended in the Congo country, where he found plentiful forests and mighty rolling rivers, and had all manner of hunting to his heart's content. Back he hurried to heaven by the rift in the clouds, and at last, through curiosity more than obedience, the wife agreed to see the earth. The couple settled in Congoland, where they begat their first children. Both were godly and pious, living in perfect bliss, and their happiness was only spoiled when the evil Fire-Spirit of the forest tempted the woman to sin.

A legend similar to this is well known among

the Zulus.   Philology proves that they are the direct descendants of the *Soren*, a sept of the Santal negroes in Bengal; but the Zulus themselves hold other views.   The old warriors believed that their first ancestors lived in heaven; they were mighty hunters before the Lord.   But in their case also curiosity tempted them to earth. It was fair to look upon, and to humour them *Unkulunkulu* let them down in a basket.   From this circumstance they say they take their national name, because *zulu* means " heaven."   Such an argument is, of course, very weak, as the word has developed its present shape in recent times, whereas the legend is of antediluvian date, being claimed by other peoples (such as the Florida islanders) totally unconnected with the Zulus.

That other peoples of antiquity possessed stories like those found to-day in Zululand and the Congo Free State may be assumed from the fact that some of them were called after heaven, their place of birth, and others after God, because He was their great " Ancestor." The Assyrians took their name from *Ashur*, " God," while the Ammonites were the sons of *Ammon*, God the " Father."   Such intimate connections, taken together with the preceding folktales, lay emphasis on certain salient facts or suppositions concerning our first parents' relationship to God.   They were originally pure and perfect in the sight of God, and lived with

Him in heaven above the starry sky. But as curiosity tempted the happy pair to earth, they allowed it to loosen their connection with the upper sphere; and the woman's temptation led to the final rupture between God and man. Despite the fall and consequent degradation, the divinity of man is a fact that is never questioned by the negro. And as he came from the upper sphere, so must he return after death when he has put away his wickedness.

Value of Negro Folktale and Tradition. — Most of these legends are difficult to understand, still more to interpret. They deal with a period in human history of which the world has lost count, but which, in strictest truth, is not lost but gone before. The vanished world before the Flood is well reflected in the stories which the negro's vivacity and poetic imagination so much help to animate; and these, in turn, give way to older stories about man's previous existence in heaven. And supposing that many of them were stripped naked of imagery and exaggeration, a genuine residuum of native belief would remain undisturbed. Once the fabulous setting is gone, the main facts of Revealed Religion stand out clear and distinct; and as they live by faith alone, they can owe nothing to Natural Religion. They deal solely with persons and facts outside Nature's bounds, and neither knowledge nor experience could ever have taught the negroes to associate them with matters spiritual.

To the negro a genuine folktale is Sacred Writ. Its testimony cannot be impugned. Although he is aware of the elusiveness of its doctrines, he believes them without criticism, because his simple faith is easily satisfied. By it he is made to confess the existence of God, and if one tale about God's doings in past ages be disbelieved, he can produce a dozen others to verify its worth. His faith finds its highest and noblest expression in his folktales, and reveals to him how God is the beginning of all things, and that man is His last and greatest creation. Man, however, differs from all the other creations in that divine parentage is claimed for him; but how the negroes learned this, and believed it as early as 4000 B.C., is a question easier asked than answered. God is the Father of men because He begat them directly. The rest of Creation just "growed."

In a perfectly general way, one might suppose that all men—good, bad, and indifferent—pass into glory after death by virtue of their divine origin; but such is not the opinion of the negro. The Congo legend of the Fire-Spirit is careful to lay forcible stress on the fact that man was, originally, made perfect before God; but it is equally precise in showing how the woman sinned by secretly allowing the

Spirit of Evil to have liaison with her. As a consequence, the descendants of the first human pair, brother and sister, were not perfect, but partook in various degrees of the good and evil inherent in the different parents.

The moral of the story is lucid enough. It traces human wickedness to the evil Fire-Spirit, and, as a logical sequence, good spirits are expected to return to the upper sphere above *i-zulu*, and trouble earth no more, while bad spirits are forced by their paternity to keep company with the Fire - Spirit throughout the ages. Thus the negroes explain why they are always afraid of evil spirits which are ever present, and as they try in every possible way to appease their anger the worship of Mulungu materially suffers.

The primary tenets of negro faith are easily summed up because they are simple. Above all, religion to the negro means belief in the being of God. God is Eternity, the Great Beginner and Creator of all, and it is He who has implanted those diviner elements in man, which live apart from human ignorance and error. As He is the source and giver of life, and gave freely of His own life and being to man, man cannot die, but only the diviner elements in his nature can live through eternity.

Such is a negro's creed, and to illustrate the fundamental doctrines of his faith he can offer nothing but the evidence of folktales. It is true they have all a superficial flimsiness, but it is extrinsic rather than essential. Millions of humanity have the same tales to tell of their origin, and they are not to be despised or lightly regarded. As regards the Indo - Bantu race, the stories and parables can be traced from Zululand to Bengal, and since they are so widespread to-day negro humanity of 4000 B.C. must have had the soundest reasons for preserving them in their entirety, to be a means of human edification and a heritage for generations to come. Of a truth they are not fully understood by the negroes, simple as is the structure of the tales and the lucidity of their morals; but with the help of Gospel parables it is easy for others to read between the lines. In the beginning the Divine knowledge was imparted to the negroes, but in such an apparently simple way that its depths were never really fathomed. To the primitive negroes it was not given to know the mysteries of heaven's kingdom, so that seeing, they saw not; hearing, they heard not, nor understood the things they saw and heard.

CHAPTER II

THE ORIGIN OF DEATH

"Death is the end. Now we live; by and by we shall die; then we shall follow our fellows. He is gone; we shall never see him more; we shall never shake his hand again; we shall never hear him laugh again."—DU CHAILLU.

SUCH were the parting words which greeted the ears of the great explorer of Equatorial Africa, when he bade farewell to his dusky friends. It needs no stretch of the imagination to infer from them that negroes bore the burden of a hopeless lot, without God or belief in a future life. But the inference, however reasonable, cannot be made to square with fact. Negro religion does not thrive on atheism, nor indeed could have wielded such absolute powers over the native intellect, and flourished and spread throughout the length and breadth of Africa, unless it possessed certain elementary truths, ineradicable because they appealed to man's inner conscience and feelings. The negro's faith in God is scarce stronger than his belief in an after-life, even although both have descended from his Indian forefathers, and have not sprung up independently on African soil.

What is Death ?—Death, say the negroes
who claim a knowledge of the occult, is the
renewal of an end. It initiates a spiritual existence that knows no ending, and suffers no change
or decay. It brings the functions and energies
of matter to a close, and signifies the final triumph
of spirit over matter, because the new form of
life gives freer opportunities and wider scope for
energy. In short, death would have no terrors
for the negro whatever had ancient religion not
taught him that, in most of its forms, it comes as a
criminal punishment for human wickedness and sin.

Life does not find its excellence in the grave.
It is not matter which decays with use, but spirit
which lives in eternal youth. That is why in
Bantu speech "life" and "spirit" are synonymous terms, and death does not affect life, just
because it is spirit. When the Atonga swing
the mortal remains of a friend to and fro at the
graveside, they chant in mournful strain, "We
are leaving to-day, we follow our fellows." And
though friend follows friend to the back of
beyond, religious custom and fear compel them
to remember their dead friend in his new abodes.
Their unalterable belief that death makes no
change in life has taught them their respect for
the dead, the care of tombs, and the solicitude
with which they minister to the supposed wants
of the departed. Corporeal being is lost, they
say, but the spirit remains endowed with greater

life, energy, and power ; and it is this which goes to join the great majority,—those whom the Zulus call *ma-dhlozi*, "the people who have died, whose breath has gone out of them." These are the throng of the living dead who, once rid of the body, become possessed of great powers to work weal and woe to humankind.

The Fear of Death.—The negro fears the dead more than the living. Without a belief in life after death, he might have been less superstitious and cruel ; and without a knowledge of spirit-power, he might have had less fear. He always speaks of the departed with awe and trembling. The dead have ears to hear and eyes to see, besides the power and will to avenge. To be reticent about the dead, or name them by a periphrasis is therefore a duty rather than a virtue. Moreover, superstition has impressed on his mind the consequences of sacrilege and injury to the dead. Should a dead man hear his name disparaged, he will up and prostrate the irreverent nigger with the measles, smallpox, or some other painful malady. Only to the devil-doctor would the news bring joy, because once he learns the childhood-name of the deceased, his magic knowledge helps him to make a servant of the spirit, and bid it do his ghoulish work.

Reasons like these oblige the negro to speak well of the dead. He may not refer to them by name. He is even forbidden to say that they are dead, and thus etiquette forces him to use circumlocutions often intelligible to a negro alone. Among those less difficult to understand may be noted: " He has gone on a long journey;" "he is no more;" "he is not here;" "he will never look upon the sun again;" " he has gone home;" "he has returned to Mulungu."

It is generally supposed that the spirit ascends to heaven above the sky; and by so doing "goes home" to Mulungu.   At this stage, personal entity and character are not lost in the Being of God, since a spirit can intercede with Him on behalf of earthly friends; but after a cycle of years its mundane interests cease, and then its disappearance from human ken is explained by its passage to a higher sphere or mansion of heaven, where live the old-time forefathers of the race.

It is otherwise with the wicked spirits of men, who lack the diviner feelings which eternity can develop and improve.   They are much weaker than the good spirits, and seem to avoid them for that reason.   Yet they are more jealous of power than anything else; and if they cling to the world, it is not because humanity is as wicked as themselves, but because men are weaker, and fit objects before whom to parade their power. Thus while the good spirits of the lately dead hover about their friends for a short period of time ere they vanish, wicked spirits are vindictive, and trouble men for ages.   In the next chapter, it will be shown how the negroes fear and worship the wicked spirits of men, whose bodies died about five millenniums ago.

Forms of Death.—To say that the negro fears death is an anomaly, for to him death is a term of vague meaning.   There are at least four aspects of death, not all of which are robed in sable pall.   In the first place comes natural decay.   A man may reach the allotted span of years, then droop and die.   Such an one does not see death, and is said by the Zulus to "go home" (*ukugoduka*).   In other words, the old folks never die ; they return to their Great Parent, *Unkulunkulu*.   Hence, no mourning is held at their decease, as God has let them fulfil the time He desired them to live ; and to make lamentations then would be impious rather than the outward signs of affection.

Death from senile decay is thus not real death, but a proper and natural transition which provides for the renewal of life in the aged.   Such a change is held in no awe, because it has not the sting of real death.   "He lived to a good old age till he went home" is the Zulus' phrase, which pithily expresses their fearlessness of a natural death.

Death is a Violence.—In all other cases, death and violence are synonymous, and a reasonable cause for fear.   Murder, poisoning, suicide, and fatal accidents and diseases result in death, and all are varied forms of violence. No blame attaches to anyone when an old man dies, but a serious view is taken of other deaths. As a rule, the inquests are followed up by prosecutions, and the death traced to someone else who is killed for the supposed crime.

Were a person in the bloom of youth or middle age suddenly cut off, the explanation that would first suggest itself to the negro would be witchcraft. Some local witch or wizard would then be suspected, and if possible, the crime would be brought home. It is common knowledge that a wizard can kill his enemy by charms and in-cantations. His " Evil Eye " is enough to bring about the desired result ; and so, the wasting of the body followed by death is technically known as, among the Santals, the " Wizard Disease " (*nanjom duk*). Discovery of the criminal leads to a heavy fine being imposed, but death if his victim be rich and influential.

Belief in the Evil Eye and the wizard's power to cause death thereby has wrought sad havoc among the negroes. It has taught them to regard most forms of death as due to violence, and as such to be avenged by one or more deaths accord-ing to a man's social position. It lends itself to open injustice and cruelty, because every man suspects his neighbour, and the innocent but seldom escape. The unfortunate wretch, too poor to bribe the witch-finder, is sacrificed to private animosity or public indignation, and invariably meets a horrible death. Needless to say, the death of a young and popular chief is a grievous calamity, setting the whole countryside in a state of terror because of the likely holocaust to follow.

The third form of death is induced by spiritual agency. The Santal *nanjom*, or spiritualist, gets into communication with an evil demon which he orders to obsess his enemy. Immediately, the man is seized with the demon of some virulent disease which is said to be " eating the soul or life." The man dies, perhaps, from the disease, and as in the preceding case, his death is traced to violence. If he has friends, they will try to "drive the devil out" by whipping him, and the awful howls and yells he makes when under the scourge (*charchari*) are audible proof of the suffering devil within. And when this treatment fails, they resort to the witch-finder, who "smells out" the spiritualist, and forces him to exorcise the demon. Very seldom, however, does the discovery of the wizard lead to the patient's cure. He is too well doctored for that.

Spirits cause sickness and death by obsession, and in both instances the crime has to be traced to some human agent on account of the spirit's elusiveness. In days not so long ago, one man had to pay the penalty of another's death; but now through the Government's restraining hand in Bengal and Central Africa, native justice is satisfied with his expulsion from the village. The change is reckoned beneficial, as most think out-lawry a lesser evil to being hung and quartered, lynched, or roasted to death at the stake.

Death by the Will of God.—The fourth and last form of death is attributed to the Will of God. Against it there can be no appeal. None would defy *Unkulunkulu,* the "Almighty," as to call His acts in question; and the negro must perforce be resigned to his fate. He considers the divine act of violence to be the natural outcome of God's wrath, and in this way reveals the main source and cause of his fear of God. Mulungu is good; a beneficent Being far away, who sends showers of blessings on His children. But often He works evil. He punishes His children when they forget and neglect Him, by sending drought, famine, and pestilence. Or again, He may kill them in His wrath. Either He will choose the simple mode of killing them outright with the lightning and thunderbolt, or else adopt the slower process of afflicting their bodies with diseases which the most skilful doctors cannot cure.

When men die of infectious disease in Uganda, they are buried in the most out-of-the-way places, the dark nooks of the forest being the fittest spots to conceal the victims of divine wrath. With the Akikuyu of British East Africa, incurable diseases are all reckoned manifestations of the will of *Ngai Mwuru*, who puts the evil-doer into hysterical or epileptic fits; and in more heinous cases, sends him consumption, pneumonia, enteric fever, and other diseases beyond medical skill to alleviate or cure. In the Bondei country, anyone who dies from dropsy, smallpox, leprosy, and dysentery, is regarded as one marked out for retribution. The vials of Mulungu's wrath are poured on his head, and soon the unhappy man is deserted by friends and relations. When dead, none are left to mourn his loss. He is hurriedly buried by a single attendant, who ends his few obsequies by sacrificing a sheep and throwing its excrement over his grave. Ever after, men strive to forget him, and blot out his name and memory from their minds because he was accursed of God.

In like manner, the Zulus conceive of God in His angry moods. Through Nature's frown is seen the wrath of God, and when the tropical storms rage in all their fury, they know *Unkulunkulu* is stamping along, armed with His lightning and thunderbolts. Perchance a native sorcerer or *um-takati* is preparing medicines outside his hut to keep off the lightning from the kraal, when he is suddenly struck by a flash and killed. For him there is no sympathy. God has meted out to him the penalty of his former crimes; and as he is obviously accursed of God, he is denied the common right of burial. His body is burnt and the ashes flung into the nearest river, because if he were buried, God would be so annoyed that, at the next storm, He would cause a thunderbolt to pitch out the remains. Such is the fanciful explanation of the old custom to cremate wizards, but the Zulu habit of cremating the victim is more probably the survival of the primitive idea which supposed that the wicked soul as well as body could be annihilated together by fire.

Consumption (*xwala*) is a disease generally recognised to be incurable in Zululand; and as no doctor was ever known to confess ignorance or lack of medical skill, diseases beyond the doctor's power to cure are ascribed to divine intervention, and allowed to take their course. The sufferer resigns himself with fortitude, while his neighbours look on him with disfavour and avoid his approaches. He dies the victim of a cruel superstition for which there can be little justification.

Among other important diseases classed as incurable in Bantuland may be mentioned scrofula, sleeping-sickness, syphilis, elephantiasis, leprosy, dysentery, cancer, etc., the number and importance of which bear small testimony to the boasted skill of herbalist, medicine-man, and witch-doctor. They at least serve to throw a sidelight on negro faith; that while God is reckoned the Giver of all good, the natives have long since learned to think of Him as a dreaded Being who sends pain and sickness, — often without apparent reason, and whose anger once aroused is as sudden as it is terrible in its consequences, dragging the victim to a nameless and dishonoured grave. Of course, a righteous man might reasonably meet his death from lightning or disease, but in neither case would he escape the cruelties of negro logic and the ban of public opinion.

We need not, however, pass hasty condemnation on the negro, for, after all, did the Jews of old live any better than they, or reason more logically? Too much do we read of the "hand of the Lord" in the Old Testament, because the fear of God, through human ignorance, was allowed to obscure God's love to man. When Uzzah stumbled and accidentally touched the ark of the Lord, we are told in the sixth chapter of *Samuel* that he was at once slain by the hand of God for his unwitting error. But when God Himself comes in the person of Christ to a sinful world, all are anxious to touch but the hem of His garment. Accordingly the negro's blind fear of God is not born of superstition, but has arisen from ignorance of God's great love, even for a sinful world. Fear is a spiritual emotion begotten of helplessness, and towards God expresses the instinctive sense of retribution yet to come. If God, the Almighty consuming fire, is not allowed in this life to enter our hearts and burn out of them all wickedness and impurity with His unquenchable flame, be sure He will ultimately burn out that wickedness in the world to come. And herein lies the human sense of spiritual retribution.

God's Wrath and Curse. — What the negroes hold to-day, their fathers possessed long ago in India, as may be judged from the uniformity of Kol with Bantu belief. To the Santals of Bengal, Jehovah is *Singbonga*, perfect in nature and the source of all good. He is not a personification of the sun, as some suppose, because of His omnipotence. He is reckoned personal and invisible, the *maranguterni* or "Almighty" whom no form of greatness or majesty can excel. But He has also the attributes of evil, and His goodness departs the earth when calamity and misfortune fall upon it.

Many stories are told of the ancient days when He manifested His wrath, and punished men with plague and death for their sins. From the upper country He sent fearful pestilences which created devastation, and storms and floods which played havoc with the country bordering on the Ganges. He also rained down on the earth plagues of vermin, worms, frogs, and snakes, which dropped from the clouds in such numbers that nobody could tell their origin, or why they were so numerous and vile.

God is the bringer of misfortune and disease.
"Whom He loveth He chasteneth" is intelligible
to the negro in a contrary sense, for the negro
prefers to be left alone, and fears all his life that
some day the Nemesis of heaven may overtake
him. If the Pelasgian Apollo could send a nine
days' pestilence on the wilful Greeks, so can
Singbonga visit a whole community with plague
and disaster as well as the individual sinner.
The native knows that God's wrath is provoked
by human sin, and in the time of His displeasure,
when disease falls or the crops are blighted with
mildew and drought, the Santal will seek God
and pray for mercy. "Alas, Singbonga! Why
do you treat us so? why is your anger broken
out upon us?" he will say; and then he will hunt
up his spiritual adviser, who, for a consideration,
will intercede for him, and make due sacrifices—
at the suppliant's expense.

Should people die of an incurable complaint,
they are suspected of impiety. Their sin has
found them out, for they bear the visible marks
of God's wrath on their bodies. They are truly
under the wrath and curse of God.

The antiquity of this negro way of thinking is
testified by Strabo, who wrote of the Massagetæ
that it was their national custom to cast out from
their midst the bodies of those who died of
disease. The victims, being believed to be
guilty of impiety towards God, were denied the

right of burial, and so their bodies were left for the wild beasts to devour. Hence it becomes clear that death by lightning, the thunderbolt, plague, and incurable disease is the direct result of God's wrath. Although due to the will of God, it is a violence as much as murder, and for that reason most feared; and because what God has justified man cannot condemn, so much the more is it the object of constant dread.

The negro fear of death is thus seen to owe its being and power, not to the idea that death is to be avoided because this life ends all, but to the tenet of his religion which teaches him that death is primarily a punishment to man, and in most of its forms is an act of violence. Where this fear is absent, death is robbed of its sting; the grave, of victory. The aged and infirm never see real death, for to them it comes not as a violence, but rather a relief and release. The old man goeth to his long home, where the wicked continue troubling, but the weary find peace; while the evil that men do lives after them. It cannot be laid to rest.

Death a Renewal of Life and Youth.— Can a man see God and live? Can he die and renew his existence? These are questions variously answered by the negro according to his faith and knowledge. No man has seen God and lived to tell the tale, he will say; but his religious folktales, many of which are thousands of years old, comment on the deeds of people who lived before the Flood, and talked and walked with God in perfect freedom. Nowadays, however, one must die before they can see God; but the good spirits never come back to tell divine secrets, while the wicked have nothing whatever to reveal.

The second question is answered in the same spirit. No man now renews his earthly life once he is dead; but the people of a fabulous age did it quite frequently, until there came a woman who brought death into the world of men. The first inhabitants never tasted death, and although age brought decay in its train, God had foreordained that man was to renew his youth at recurring intervals. Legends about men and women renewing their youth are to be traced from Bengal to Ireland and Zululand. It remains to show the probable steps of reasoning by which the negro may have arrived at the doctrine of Renewal of Youth.

At first the negroes thought death a very strange phenomenon. Everything they saw in Nature was governed by law and reason. The sun rose and set; the stars twinkled the same; and the earth, with its forests, hills, seas, and rivers, never seemed to decay and die. But one little planet was unlike all these. The moon, with its phases, was observed from the earliest ages because it helped men to measure time. It was a visible timepiece, with beings inside to regulate the face of the clock; but regarded in the light of a person, the moon was the most human of planets. It was lazy by day, habitually kept late hours, and on going home made faces in the small hours of the morning. When young it was little, but waxed bigger and stronger as its brightness grew. At Full Moon it was in the prime of life, thereafter drooping till it faded and disappeared. "It is dead" (*is'ifile*), say the Zulus, who, like other negro tribes, mourn the old moon's death till the New Moon appears.

Viewed in this way, the moon becomes the sole emblem of change and decay, time and death. It is compared to a crafty old woman who kills people she wants to eat, and being so intimately associated with darkness and the powers of evil, is greatly feared for its witchcraft and the deaths that it causes. Above all, it is the "Light of the Dead," and when it first appears and is last visible, the negroes say they are most likely to die.

All Bantu traditions affirm that the moon really lives and dies, but it is different from men of to-day in that it renews its youth once a month. The New Moon is genuine; not a mere re-appearance of the old; nor is it derived from matter supplied by the dead and worn-out orb. Yet it was clear from the beginning that the New Moon was not everlasting like the sun and

earth, but renewed its life and youth immediately
after death ; and so, by the force of analogy, men
came to think that they too died and renewed
their life and youth. Unhappily, they die nowadays and never return, and thus nobody is sure
whether a man dies and renews his existence in
other parts of the world. "Men do not know,
and the spirits have never told."

The appearance of the New Moon is the signal
for rejoicing among the negroes. Their favourite
luminary is restored to the haunts of men. Life
has conquered death. In the Congo "Free"
State the time of New Moon begins the revelry by
night, and Belgium's colonial beauty and wisdom
gather to the sound of tom-tom, flute, and soft
recorder. Men bring out their household gods
and idols, and honour them with a new coat of
paint. Then they fall on their knees and clap
their hands and cry, "So may I renew my life as
thou art renewed!" The Bahima of Uganda
come out of their huts, clap their hands in salute
to the moon, and wish each other health, wealth,
and prosperity through the ensuing month. The
salute of the Wagogo, in German East Africa, is
to fire off guns, blow horns, beat drums, and in
general to make a joyful noise. Like other Bantu
tribes, they do not worship any heavenly body,
but honour the New Moon for the principle it
upholds. By their public rejoicings they express
to all and sundry their hopes that, as it has taken

a new lease of life, so may they renew their life and health. Hence they often greet the New Moon with the fervent prayer that all illness may go to the west where the sun sets.

Much evidence might be brought to bear on the subject of life-renewal as illustrated by the moon, but the opinion of Mungo Park may be taken as conclusive about negro belief. He wrote that negroes looked upon the moon as a new creation, and, at its appearance, thanked God for His goodness. " This prayer is pronounced in a whisper—the party holding up his hands before his face; its purpose (as I have been assured by many different people) is to return thanks to God for His kindness through the existence of the past moon, and to solicit a continuation of His favour during that of the new one."

The superstition about the moon's rejuvenescence was not unknown to antiquity, as we find Strabo relating it of the negro population of Spain. On the appearance of every New Moon, said he, whole families passed the night dancing and feasting. As they stood before their doors they made solemn sacrifice to their "nameless god," who must undoubtedly have been none other than Jehovah and not the moon, since Jehovah of the negroes is addressed solely by his titles or attributes, but is otherwise "nameless," from the absence of the indefinite term "God."

Resurrection of the Dead.—Applying the phases of the moon to their own case, the negroes see nothing illogical in the doctrine of rejuvenescence. It is these which have led them to conceive, perhaps, of the change and renewal of life and the resurrection of the dead. But there is a marked divergence between the two. The renewal of life and youth is the natural condition induced by death; the resurrection of the dead is an act of witchcraft which any skilful necromancer can perform by magic. Thus it happens that in native folktales the same men get killed over and over again, but are rejuvenated again rather than raised from the dead. The aged hero gets killed in the first chapter, but turns up whole and hearty in the next. Even Homer was consistent in this respect.

An illustration will serve to show how the magic of some folktales owes its being to religious principles, which it tries to explain darkly. A Ugandan tale speaks of a godlike man called Wabulenkoko, who came down from heaven to dwell among men; and the various times he is killed and renews his life form the episodes and thrilling scenes. In the first incident he is seized by the king of Uganda and put to death without trial, but immediately after appears before the king. He is next cut to pieces and his body burnt; but this availed nothing, as he walked out of the fire and arrived at the king's court before his executioners. A deep grave is then dug, and spears placed erect in it with skins stretched over them. Wabulenkoko is lowered into the grave, and the earth firmly stamped down so that he could not get out; but the executioners flew into fits when they saw their victim had reached home long before them. However, the hero had tasted enough of the milk of human kindness, and wanted no more; so, after rating the king soundly, he ascended to heaven and worked out his revenge. Soon, he sent down a stormy rain of fire which burned all the houses and singed the king badly. The king thereupon took to his heels, and, by an undignified flight, saved himself a horrible death. He prayed Wabulenkoko to forgive him for all the injuries he had done him in the flesh, and to send no more of his fire-rains. Ever after, he feared him devoutly, and honoured him with the choicest sacrifices and gifts.

The Uganda legend is of much interest from the way it illustrates several points of negro belief. Like many of its kind, it speaks freely of the days of man when God lived on the earth, and why He returned to heaven and sent the fire-rains. As in the Tale of the Chameleon, stress is laid on the belief that God was hated of men, and it was from the persecution of hate more than anything else that He left the earth for ever. Finally, the story shows to perfection what the renewal of life signifies. As regards

Wabulenkoko, it illustrates the inherent power of God or Christ to rise from the dead, physically unchanged or uninjured by death in any form.

Lunar rejuvenescence, in reality, seems to be a negro theory which attempts to justify rather than prove the belief that death is the renewal of life, the beginning of an end.   It leaves unexplained how the negroes came to think of a spiritual life beyond the grave, to contemn death except in its violent forms, and to learn of and define the various stages in the spiritual life. The phases of the moon is a theory too inelastic to prove the truth of the eternity of life.   This the negroes know full well when they explain it away by saying that times have changed, and men do not renew their life as of yore.   But in the battle of faith with theory, faith conquers reason, and thus no doubt ever shakes the negro mind that Life conquers Death.   From the broken strands of Death itself is woven the endless web of Life.

Instincts of the Soul.—Something must be said about the negro's philosophy of death. Sleep is closely allied to death because it extracts the soul, but without injuring the body.   It is a natural form of death inducing temporary unconsciousness, and does not affect either mental or bodily activity.   On the contrary, death, the brother of sleep, "son of the sable night," makes the body supine and motionless, and stops the heart where the spirit or life is centred. The Wagogo call death a "sleep," and sleep a "little death." The Yaos also call it a sleep, and think that sleep and death are twins because so like each other.

In Uganda, natives speak of death as "that which turns the heart" (*kukyusa mutima*), the local superstition being that the heart is like a bag or casket open at one end which, when turned upside down by death, allows the life to escape. Thereafter, the spirit goes to the place of the departed, and renders its account to Walumbe in the next world. Death in this light becomes synonymous with spiritual liberation, a freedom from physical weakness and restraint.

Negro idiom often expresses in epigrammatic form many local ideas and beliefs. The Zulus differentiate between the qualities of mind and heart, as they do between faith and reason. The head they hold to be the seat of knowledge, and the heart the source of the passions and affections according as the "life" within transmits them. What we learn "by heart," the Zulus and Basques learn "by head" (Zulu *ngo kanda* = Basque *buruz*), because the life is not reason, and cannot make itself understood by mere ideas of knowledge. Rather is it endowed with instinct which, totally unlike human reason, is not confined by mental and physical restrictions. By its aid, witch-doctors can forecast the future, their success as prophets varying with their powers of instinct. Common people have very little instinct, as they never develop it; but they are reminded of its existence sometimes, when a nameless feeling in their nature warns them of coming events. The Zulus will then say that their heart tells them of calamities in store by reason of its unwonted palpitations, and if any-one is suddenly troubled with what he calls "palpitation of the heart," he will exclaim that his heart is thinking of someone. *Namhlanje intliziyo indwemele ekaya*, "To-day my heart has been thinking of home," is what a Zulu says when instinct tells him that something untoward has happened in his home or kraal. Moreover, the negro can tell, by means of his heart, if a request has been granted or prayer refused. In either case, the instinct is affected with elation or sadness long before the man himself discovers the reason.

It is the heart that expresses the emotions of the soul. When people are quick-tempered (as slow people usually are), they are said to have a "short heart" (*intliziyo imfushane*). When a man first discovers himself a fool, he puts on "side" to convince his neighbours of his superior worth; and in this country, we say he is suffering from "swelled head." The Zulus, on the other hand, say he has "swelled heart" (*intliziyo nkulu*), because the emotion which produces egotism is dictated by the foolish instinct of the spirit. Similarly, a covetous man is one whose heart is always saying *Lobilobi, Lobilobi,* "Come, come and be mine!"

The Coming of Death.—About the coming of death there are only traditions. What time death came first into the world of man is outside negro calculation, but how and why it came are questions that seldom go unanswered. Most of the folktales agree that a woman was the cause of the mischief, since, I suppose, wherever there is evil and temptation there a woman will be.

Once on a time, say the Yaos, when the world was young, people never died, until there came along a woman weak and deformed. In her travels she discovered one night two men fast asleep and snoring loudly, and curious to see what would happen, ventured to hold the nostrils of one of the sleepers. He never awoke. Next morning his friends tried to wake him, and shouted and danced, but it was of no use; and then it dawned on them that something new had surely come amongst them when the sleeper would not waken. So he was left to sleep, and ever since the old folks who go off to sleep and forget to waken are truly said to have gone off to the land of Nod.

A version from Uganda resembles this in the way it attributes death to the evil curiosity

inherent in feminine nature. In the beginning,
God sent Kintu, the father of the Baganda, from
the upper country, and loaded him with one of
each kind of animal and vegetable that he might
need on earth. Now his brother Walumbe, the
Spirit of Death, hated him, and intended to
waylay and kill him as soon as he left the
" Plains of Abraham" above. But God knew
of Walumbe's hate as well as Kintu's frailties;
and to give the latter his only chance of escape,
advised him to start very early for earth in the
morning, and never return to heaven for anything
he might forget. Putting his bundle on his
shoulder, Kintu bravely set out with his wife,
and made tracks for Uganda. But, alas! The
day was well advanced when his wife found that
she had forgotten the small grains of *mbulo* for
feeding the hens. Setting Kintu's better judgment at naught, she hied back to heaven as fast
as she could, and got from God the grains she
wanted. Then she returned to Kintu, but not
alone, for hard in her footsteps hastened the
wrothful Spirit of Death whom Kintu had hood-
winked in the morning. Through a disobedient
woman Death learned the road to the earth,
and ere long repaid her kindness by shooting
and killing her children.

The Congo legend on the Origin of Man,
referred to in the previous chapter, which shows
how the first man and woman came to earth

from heaven, thus proceeds :—The man was out hunting one day in the forest when he ran across an awful demon. He saw no hope of escape, but, fortunately, the demon did not try to injure him. When he got home he told his wife about his adventure with the Fire-Spirit, the Demon of Death, and warned her to steer clear of the locality. His warning, unfortunately, whetted her curiosity the more, till at last she determined to see if the demon was so terrible as her husband said. Chance offered one day when her "mere man" was hunting, and she stole away to the forest. The Fire-Spirit appeared, but as a stately youth more handsome than her bearded husband, and so fascinated her with his beauty and silvery tongue that before they parted they fell in love and made liaison together. The woman then hurried home, and never told her husband of her adventure with the Fire-Spirit. After some months she bore two children to her husband, who was astonished beyond measure to find one child bright and innocent-looking, and the other dark-browed and of repulsive appearance. Not till then did he know of his wife's sin and shame ; and it was this woman's disobedience and sin that brought death to mankind, because the evil child carried the seed of the Spirit of Death in his body, and so contaminated the good child that both transmitted the seed of death to all their posterity.

The Fall of Man.—Most negro legends associate the name of the first woman with the Spirit of Death, and almost seem to justify the degraded social state of women on the plea that the first of them dragged innocent man down with her from the paths of virtue and hopes of heaven. As those from Nyassaland, Uganda, and the Congo tend to show, death was the punishment for a woman's sin. It was not originally decreed to man, being more than mere animal decay, but was caused by woman disobeying the laws of God, who thereupon signed the death-warrant of the human race.

A more popular class of tales shifts the responsibility of sin from the woman to lower animals. Doubtless Adam quarrelled with his wife when he realised the consequences of her sin to him and his children; but it seems that he received from her such a curtain lecture that he never reproved her again. So, with becoming modesty, Adam learned to explain to the family how various animals brought death to man by their sins. A folktale, well known throughout South Africa, describes how the moon once sent an insect to men with the message: "As I die and dying live, so ye shall also die and dying live." The insect proved to be a local "Weary Willie," and was overtaken on the road by the hare, who persuaded it to give him the message because he was a faster runner. The insect gladly consented, but the hare repeated the message so often to himself on the road that he got confused, and delivered it thus : "As I die and dying perish, in the same way ye shall also die and perish." The hare thereafter returned to the moon and told her what he had said, but so incensed was she at the hare's audacity and folly that she flew after him with an axe and struck him on the lip. Since that day the hare has gone about with a slit lip, and when reproved for being so hare-brained, is as mad as a March hare to deny it.

In most Central African tales, the hare gives place to the lizard or chameleon, but legends differ according to locality. The version of the Angoni Zulus runs, that in the beginning God ordered the chameleon to tell men that they would die and rise again. On second thoughts, He changed the divine plan, and sent the grey lizard to tell them that they would die and never return to earth. The chameleon was in no hurry, whereas the common lizard made neither stop nor stay till he unburdened himself of God's message. Soon after, the chameleon came snailing into the kraal, and told the villagers what God had commanded. But men drove him out without a hearing. "We have received the word of the lizard," said they, "and now we cannot take yours." For this reason the negroes hate the chameleon, and stuff its mouth with snuff, delighted to watch its dying agonies wherever it is found. It brought death to us, they say; it had no right to delay.

In some versions of the tale, notably those of the Yao and Manganja from Nyassaland, the lizard is displaced by the salamander; but except for the local colouring the tale is the same everywhere. In all, the incidents are alike; the salamander arrives first, and the chameleon finds time to rue delay. Where the lower creation is concerned, death is brought to man by the procrastination or disobedience of some animal or insect; and it comes as a punishment to man however innocent of guilt. Both types of tale are therefore one and the same, with slight modifications. Both teach the lesson that man at first knew not death in its true sense, and that death was a punishment for disobedience, either on the part of the woman or that of an animal towards God. The moral in both types of tale is so clear that even he who runs may read. Sin is primarily a transgression towards God, and of sin death is the fruit.

The Wages of Sin.—To give a definition of sin from a negro point of view is a very difficult matter. Native custom is always the determining factor, and as times change the virtues of one age often become vices in the next. Lying is not a sin, and even the pious Jews of old held a like opinion; otherwise the Ten Commandments would have denounced it as strongly as Christ did. Neither is drunkenness a vice, but rather a proof of wealth and social standing, since only the rich can afford to keep drunk for any length of time. Theft is but a proof of dexterity. To steal from one's enemies is a virtue, but to steal from one's neighbours and friends is proved to be a vice, especially when the thief is caught. From this way of thinking, the negro has led himself to distinguish vice from virtue according as his sentiments or prejudices may influence his mind. In short, the sin that injures one's friends becomes a virtue when committed against enemies.

Certain sins against an individual or community are never lightly condoned. Incest, adultery, rape, murder, arson, witchcraft, and flagrant breaches of public morals or offences against the chief, are punished by death, but lighter crimes are overlooked if fines are paid.

To these have to be added the sins of hypocrisy and a lack of humility. For the former, God once killed a woman with His bottles of lightning, and for the latter He disappointed men in their quest for fire. These sins are denounced only in folktales; and folktales do not interpret the spirit of a modern age nor reflect its morals. In them alone do the sins of hypocrisy and pride, procrastination and disobedience, obtain such prominence, all the more remarkable because to-day no significance is attached to them. The heinousness of such sins belongs, therefore, to some remote age, and to a state of society with a code of morals far above that of the modern negro. It is to that ancient age of virtue that the folktales of the negro really belong.

Vice is a term of relative value, and serious only as the individual or age chooses to regard it. Sin is differently defined, because it is against God, and on that account always heinous. A man may lead a life of vice without injuring his neighbours, or indeed without their knowledge, but if he is struck with lightning or some fatal disease, they at once know he is guilty of secret sin against God. And it is because of that sin he must die by violence. Being under His wrath and curse, he is a condemned criminal, accursed openly of God, to become an outcast from his fellow-men.

Death by the will of God for human sin is justified because God is just, and there is no appeal beyond Mulungu. But as wizards and witches can induce death, and are anything but virtuous, it follows that the deaths they cause cannot be justified. The witch may kill the victim of her spleen, but as such death is the result of malice, it is another form of murder. Thus is it rendered necessary to hunt out and kill witches and wizards who weave the ruin of men. They punish their enemies with death on account of their hate, and select some form of violent death, which is the severest penalty they can exact.

Ignoring altogether the legends and superstitions which prove that the average magician regards death as a punishment, there stands forth a religious principle which not all the amount of negro superstition can obscure. Death is a violence and a severe form of punishment to men, and is the wages of sin if induced by the Will of God.

From the foregoing facts and arguments, it is plain that the negroes have defined death, its origin and cause, to their own satisfaction. Strictly speaking, death finds no place in the native creed, which, indeed, recognises it only as a force or state dissociated from the world of life or spirit. It has no religious importance in the folktales, because these are the antediluvian parables which teach the Word of God; and the Word of God in all ages has taught mankind to regard death as of secondary moment. The negro's fearlessness, as we have seen, is the direct outcome of his faith, not of superstition and ignorance; and if he fears death other than that brought on by old age, it is through the old religion instilling into his mind the idea that such death is unnatural, and either murder or some form of violence which is generally the meed of sin.

Atonement for Sin.—It would be out of place to take negro folktales as hard truth, and unscientific to pass them over altogether. Whether in India or Africa, they are of uniform type, and convey one and all the lesson that man was reduced to a state of sin and misery through a woman's guilt. They agree in their views about God and His home in heaven, and uphold the divinity of man in the way they assume as unquestionable fact that man lived in heaven before God finally transplanted him to earth. Man was originally perfect before God, and it was not intended that he should die like the beasts who were formed on earth. God taught him all manner of knowledge, and how to speak and write; but his Fall from virtue changed everything, as God could no longer be the earthly companion of vice. Yet although man fell from his high estate, through no personal fault or sin of his own, but rather that of the woman, and although God hid His face from him and was seen no more, the old folktales seem to show that He was still forgiving even if He first exacted heavy penalties for sin.

This is made clear by the significance attached to the doctrine of Atonement, by which man was refused the favour of God until he put away his sin, and atoned for them by voluntary fasting, penance, and sacrifice. Atonement for sin is part of all faiths, but, while innocent in itself, has among the negroes evolved one of the bloodiest rites ever known to the ancient or modern world—the wholesale sacrifice of young children, to atone for human sin, and thereby appease the wrath of God. Such is negro atonement pushed to its logical extreme; degraded some may say, and yet justified on the part of the negroes because afterwards exceeded by Christ, the Son of God, who voluntarily made the last sacrifice to His Father for the saving of the nations. By this greatest of sacrifices, Christ supported the demand of the old religion for atonement by the shedding of innocent blood; and justified the faith of millions of negroes who believed that their first ancestors brought death by sin; and felt that God, who had departed from them, was not to be approached till due atonement for sin was made.

Stages of Spiritual Life.—Negroes live in such constant fear of the other world that it would be unwise to ignore as valueless their ideas of the after-life. Death is supposed to belong to the material world only; hence its coming is spiritual liberation. Further than this, there is no change. The life or spirit remains untouched, is human, and is bereft neither of sex, feelings, nor interests. Very few spirits, however, trouble the earth save the lately dead, and the wicked who cannot undo the evil they have done in the body; while those who do not depart soon to the higher realms of Mulungu cling to the cares of this world, and are racked with pain and pleasure, grief and joy,—a nuisance to themselves and a terror to humanity.

Save the wicked, who have nothing to gain by a change of existence, spirits do not mourn their departure from earth; but, according to the Santal or Zulu negro, exception is made for mothers who die when their children are in infancy. They are believed to come back at night, and watch and weep tenderly over their helpless babes. In negro fancy, it seems, maternal love is the only human instinct which would break the barriers of death if it could. And whatever value we like to attach to such a superstition, it proves the negro to have a higher opinion of maternity than most people imagine.

The chief sorrow which is said to afflict evil-minded spirits is the lack of reverence. They want to be worshipped like Mulungu, and not to be slighted like nobodies. From negro arguments, one would assume that the chief quality death instils into them is presumption and arrogance. They are more solicitous about earthly attentions than the good; and as primitive man was always anxious to soothe their passions and calm their jealousies, he did so in the only way that appealed to himself—by giving presents of beer, flour, and other offerings as he could afford. By these a spirit was pleased because the act was a mark of worship and respect; while on the other side, the giver came to look on the spirits as intensely human in their wants and feelings.

An angry spirit was a hungry spirit, the invisible agent of evil living in poverty, hunger, and thirst, and requiring to be fed with sacrifices, offerings, and other kinds of religious medicine. Among the Kols, the chief spiritual woes are hunger and thirst, both of which offerings of fowls and rice-beer materially help to allay. Many hold that a spirit is also naked, because the local witch-doctors say that spirits of ancestors appear in this guise to their sight; and thus Santal custom demands that rags of cloth be hung on branches, and at wells near which a spirit resides, or burnt on the funeral pyre so that the deceased may have the wherewithal in the next world to clothe himself.

To feed the ancestors amounts to filial duty rather than absolute necessity. The Baganda explain their position thus. Whenever the living *mwoyo* becomes a *muzimu* or disembodied spirit, it has to endure pain, hunger, cold, and other discomforts; but as its power is greater after death, and its energies and passions less restricted by physical barriers, its favour ought to be gained as a matter of self-interest. To incur displeasure is sure to bring sickness and misfortune, and these in turn are likely to end in death unless the witch-doctor interposes.

The Zulu Land of the Dead is *Tunzela*, "place of shadows"; but unsubstantial as the name appears, their fear of the shadows is very real. To captivate them, presents of beer are regularly made, and sometimes a bullock is sacrificed for their benefit. By the "shadow" is meant the life or spirit; hence the peculiar phrase applied to the dying—"His shadow is still present." Similarly, the Yaos and Manganja of Nyassaland show in their customs their terror of hungry spirits. After selecting a piece of forest-ground for a cemetery, they put the burnt clay cooking-pots of the dead near the graves. Holes are drilled in the bottoms, not so much to render them useless to the living as to allow the offerings of flour and beer to sink through to the dead man below. The countless holed grave-pots in negro-land are proof positive of the negroes' rooted belief that the spirits need and demand nurture because they are still human.

Along with many other beliefs to the same effect, customs as these show that, in negro estimate, death brings no end to human suffering and joy. Indeed, it seems that wicked spirits are subject in acuter form to the woes and ills they endured on earth. Their anger is moved by that suffering, and against weaker humanity it is directed. To satisfy, therefore, their craving for the good things of this life and obtain their goodwill, spirits must be fed. The state after death is accordingly held to be little different from earthly existence. Death changes the finite in nature, but touches not the infinite and spiritual; and so the life on earth determines the negro's state of existence in the other world. If he has been wicked, death will not remove from his nature the stains of guilt and impurity, for which he will have to spend eternity with the bands of wandering spirits who can find no rest; and who, because they continue to work evil, dislike the good and fear to meet Mulungu.

Sex of the Spirit.—Last argument of all that ends this strange eventful history of negro belief is that dealing with sexual recognition after death. A religious ceremony which can be traced back for about five thousand years, and of peculiar import, is bound up with the symbolism of the obol. The area over which it can be traced is certain proof, in the first place, of its genuineness and antiquity; and in common with the belief in the Fire-Spirit aforementioned, it seems to belong primarily to that Papuan substratum of thought which underlies a good deal of negro superstition.

A primitive example of its kind may be illustrated from the folklore of the Malanaus of Borneo. "The road leading to Elysium is guarded by a ferocious double-headed dog, named Mawiang, to whom it is necessary to present a valuable bead. This bead is always carefully

fastened to the right arm of a corpse, with whom
are buried gold ornaments, weapons, gongs, and
rich clothes for use in the other world, and at
whose tomb it was formerly the practice to bind
a slave, or sometimes as many as ten slaves, who
were left thus to perish that their spirits might
wait upon their master."[1]   Other Papuan and
Polynesian tribes have still more vivid stories
about Cerberus, Charon, Hades, and the path
and boat of the dead, and to the Papuan regions
are to be traced the source and genesis of such
kind of primitive lore.

Ere the Egyptian civilisation rose above its
Bantu predecessor in the land, the same habit of
fastening a bead or bracelet on the right arm of
a corpse was observed.   Further, it has been noted
that the body usually reclined on its left side,
with the face to the west, the head to the south,
and feet to the north.   In some cases, the body
in the grave-pots or urns had been completely
dismembered before burial, and the limbs artifi-
cially arranged.   This shows that *rigor mortis*
had, from some reason or another, been allowed
to set in before the body was doubled up for
inhumation, as may be verified from negro usage.
The Bantu of to-day are always very careful to
double up a dying man into the crouching
posture, and this is done before death while the
body is still warm.   In exceptional cases where

[1] *Journ. Anthrop. Inst.*, vol. v. page 35.

this is not done immediately, and *rigor mortis* sets in before the operation is completed, the body has to be cut up to suit the native mode of burial.   The Bawenda in the north-west corner of the Transvaal are known to cut the knees and elbows of the deceased until the body can be brought into the desired position.   But ordinarily, when the dead negro is too big for his coffin, " Double him up! Double him up!" is the undertaker's cry.

All over the negro area, the ceremony of fastening a bracelet, bead, or coin to the right arm of a male corpse and the left of a female has been observed from time immemorial.   The corpse reclines in a huddled-up position on the left arm and the bead is tied to the right, while in the case of females the exact opposite holds good.   Many Indian tribes, however, who burn their dead, think the tying of the bracelet to be useless, and so the ceremony is slightly altered although its significance remains.   The stone, bead, or coin is put in the mouth of the corpse ; but the other mode is followed by tribes like the Badagas of the Nilgherry Hills, who bury their dead, and are careful to tie a coin or bead round a man's right arm if he is unable to swallow it before death.   In the funeral ceremonies of the Todas, a married woman has a leafy branch put in her grave-clothes, and balls of thread and cowry-shells are tied on the arm of the corpse just above the elbow. Mr. Thurston, in his informative work on Southern India, has neglected to notice which arm the Todas prefer; but at anyrate he mentions the obol custom among them; and since the neighbouring Badagas tie it on the right arm of a male, doubtless, in Todaland also, the obol or bead may have been anciently fastened to the man's right arm and the woman's left to distinguish the sexes after death.

The observance of the same custom in Bantuland is the same as in India, because it is of Indian origin. In Uganda, when the king's body is embalmed, it is usual to keep it for two months before the remains are finally disposed of. A number of men and women are then killed to accompany and serve the deceased monarch, the men being buried on the right of the corpse and the women on the left. Among the Wagogo, the death ceremonies include the washing and anointing of the corpse, and doubling-up of the limbs. A new cloth is wrapped round it and ornaments taken off; all except an iron bracelet which is removed to the right wrist if the man's bracelet happened to be on the left before death. Should the deceased have no iron bracelet, one composed of white beads is put on his right wrist. With women the bracelet is put on the left, but the meaning of the custom is not clear to the natives. Their fathers taught them, and they follow their fathers. Men are buried reclining on the right side and women on the left.

Superstition among the Zulus attributes to this bracelet or obol powers of magic. It is called *um-nembo*, or "shell," and is believed to give its wearer the power of always hitting the mark. This peculiarity of the obol fetish recalls the old Papuan ideas about its wonderful properties. To the Fijian it suggests at once the soul's long journey over the Path of the Shades. The obol is given to the deceased to soothe the double-headed dog which lurks on the path waiting to attack them; or sometimes, as other Papuan traditions affirm, it is given to the soul for the purpose of hitting a certain tree or object with it. When the soul strikes the mark with its bead or obol, its escape from further misery is assured; if it misses its aim, untold tortures have to be undergone.[1]

Evidence of Archæology.—This old negro ceremonial spread as far as Great Britain. It has often been remarked by Bateman and others who toiled amongst the British barrows, that the skeletons of males lay on their right sides and those of females on the left. This being so, it becomes evident that the Basques of Britain made a difference in the mode of burial according to the sex of the deceased. For example, at Middleton-by-Youlgrave, in Derbyshire, a barrow

[1] Vide *Journ. Anthrop. Inst.*, vol. xxiv. pp. 350-6.

was found some time ago containing the skeleton
of a young female. It was in a doubled-up
posture, lying on the left side, and beside it lay a
highly ornamented cup of red clay, with a broken
instrument of flint. Another female skeleton,
unearthed at Bole Hill, Blakewell Moor, was also
in the contracted posture on the left side, and
surrounded by small stones. In the North Riding
of Yorkshire, near Pickering, the skeleton of an
adult female was brought to light. The knees
were drawn up to the chin and the back bent in
semi-circular form. It too reclined on the left
side. At the long barrow of Top Low, near
Swinscoe, skeletons of male adults were described
as lying on their right sides in a contracted
position. At Broad Low Ash, in Staffordshire
a barrow, when opened, displayed to view the
skeletons of two males lying on the right side,
surrounded by numerous small flint ornaments.
Such is part evidence from English barrows
about an old British Basque custom and belief.

Barrows in Scotland have been opened from
time to time, and in most the skeletons are found
in the crouched position, this being the negro
mode still followed in the disposal of the dead.
One skeleton was found upside down. It was
obviously that of an old joke-editor, who had
been much upset by the fall of the roof. Not
always are skeletons seen in the undisturbed state
as in the barrow opened at Dunrobin Park,

6

Sutherlandshire. The stone cist contained the skeleton of a lady of about nineteen summers. She was alone and unmarried. Her knees had been drawn up to the chin, but the native mat which once covered her bones had vanished into thin air, and, "like an unsubstantial pageant faded, left not a rack behind." Behind the body there were eighteen quartzose pebbles, and at the feet one hundred and eighteen small shale discs, six of which were perforated. This was not the young 'ady's wealth, although she appears to have been the daughter of a poor chieftain who ruled the Mackay country in the days of Basque dominion. All that they really intend to convey is that the old British Basque method of reckoning time was the same as that among the negroes. Taking this for granted, the age of the young Basque lady was eighteen years, four lunar months, six days. Her skull, when measured, had a cephalic index of 82.4 and nasal index 51.1 ; so on craniometrical grounds, the daughter of the Mackay chief was a worthy scion of the Caledonians, a sept of the German Basques.

On archæological grounds it has been attempted to prove that all over the negro area differences were made in the forms of burial according to sex, and that by consequence they had a religious meaning which the modern negroes have largely forgotten. The bracelet or obol is, of course, originally Papuan, but its significance is not yet lost, and, as has been shown, relates to the passage of the soul to the other world. Ancient and modern negro custom and belief being therefore taken together, one finds that two distinct ideas about an after-life stand clear. Death is the beginning of a long journey which human friends try a little to alleviate in various ways. It robs no one of humanity and unsexes none.

CHAPTER III

" Heaven bursts her azure gates to pour
Her spirits to the midnight hour."

Spiritualism.—There are no negro tribes to be found anywhere so debased and ignorant as to disbelieve in the existence of spirits. While with most the worship of Mulungu has been neglected, that of the spirits has risen in importance; and the clever medium who can impose on his fellow-men is esteemed more worthy than the man who would free them from the chains of slavery and superstition. Thus has it come to pass that the barren truths which Spiritualism teaches have, in the course of ages, degraded the negro and enfeebled his mind. The old and purer religion is liable to suffer from a species of spiritism which, although it too upholds the truth of the eternity of life, cannot elevate, because its doctrines are vague, and not always self-consistent. Nor can it administer comfort to those seeking it, when it reveals so clearly that most spirits seeking communion with men are evil. The good are ill persuaded to return to human haunts of vice and woe.

Spiritualism, better understood by the negroes than it is among us, is usually styled with them demon-worship, both being one and the same, with the same end in view—to get into communion with the spirits of the dead. Both are alike in that they appeal to curiosity rather than any pious sentiment or principle; and both end alike, because they degrade the neophyte who is so foolish to accept a false and hollow semblance of belief for true religion, of which Spiritualism is scarce the shadow. Neither of these can be made to work together in harmony, on account of the difference in their natures. The one lays undue stress on the existence of spirit after death, ignoring the fact that eternity of life to man is of itself a valueless asset. The other is practical and utilitarian in the way it appeals to man in this world. It attempts to educate him for the next by raising his morals and increasing his faith. That duty, as performed by the old negro religion, was approved by Christianity, which followed in its steps. Although, like Spiritualism, it taught the eternity of life, it gave to man an Example by which to guide his present life so that he could attain perfection in the next. If that difference be rightly grasped, it will be easier to understand why negro spiritualism and religion should not be confused. The one inspires fear and the other faith.

Nature of the Spirit.—Spirit and body are held to be two elements with nothing in common, save that the one can permeate the other, through which the character of the spirit is revealed. The former is the life which has being, power, and energy; the latter is the temporary material used for a brief space and then flung away. As the body decays with age, the life loses its hold by slow degrees, but does not itself shrink; and after it leaves, the body is deprived of energy, which only the life supplies. It is then dead and of no more use. Logically, it follows that spirit might return to a dead body and reanimate it; but although the negroes think the spirit can leave the body when it likes—as during sleep, fainting fits, slight illness, and suspended animation—no man has been able to tell what force or law prevents the spirit's return to a corpse. All they know is that to do so is against the law of God; and thus only the witches and wizards are guilty of resurrecting the dead to aid and abet their wicked schemes.

Primitive negro religion, as seen among the Kols of Bengal, consists of three different cults, all spiritual in nature. The native Jehovah is *Singbonga*, who lives far away, and being seldom angry is little feared. The natives do not pay him overmuch regard, since, like other men, they respect those of whom they are most afraid. They find greater need to appease the lesser but more volatile spirits, who are ever ready to do mischief, and delight in persecuting those they hate. Taken in inverse order, these three cults may be shortly put as follows :—

Worship of Aboriginal Spirits.
Worship of Ancestors.
Worship of God.

Fairies and Fairy-Worship.—Spirits are usually named according to their virtues and vices, power and social position. The general term is *Bonga*, the Spirit-being which survives a man's death, and enters on a new and freer existence. As it leaves the body, it takes away all spiritual faculties like consciousness of being, the emotions, character, and such intelligence and instinct that man may have possessed. In the Land of Shadows, death is supposed to bring to the good spirit a feeling of exhilaration, while in the bad it creates a feeling of vindictiveness which time cannot assuage. More especially to the latter class does the term *bonga* apply. Etymologically, it is derived from a Santal root meaning "to sacrifice," and, metaphorically, "to praise"; and in the latter sense it is found in Zulu as *bonga*, "to praise, extol"—whence *bongo*, formerly "spirit," but now applied in a technical sense to denote a tribal or totem name. "Spirit" is thus seen to be literally "that which is praised and sacrificed unto," because of the fear it inspires in man. It is perhaps superfluous to add that the Basque equivalent to Zulu *bongo* should be *pukha*; but although this term has been displaced by other synonyms, the proper word must have been familiar to the Basques of Britain in the local forms of " Puck " and " Pyxie,"—in other words, a "fairy" or spirit. The fairies of our ancestors were, after all, nothing but the spirits of the dead.

Another general term, but of infrequent use in Santali, is *buru*. Being of very ancient date and obscure in meaning, it is often found attached to the previous word as *buru-bonga*; but apart from this it is commonly met with in the names of spirits of hills, rocks, rivers, and wells—*e.g.*, *Kambru Buru* and *Hara Buru*. As a name of evil omen, it is connected etymologically with Basque *morrode*, " demon, familiar - spirit "; but as the Santals sometimes call Jehovah *Marang Buru*, "Great Spirit," it is scarce likely that the term *buru* was originally applied to demons and familiar spirits.

Tradition has been very unkind to the mischievous *bonga*, not only because he is wicked, but because his nose is of abnormal length,— meant, doubtless, to "smell out" his victims the easier. The *bongas* of India are every whit as wicked as the fairy Pucks of Britain. They come to market unseen, and steal the tradesmen's goods; get inside a fiddle, and lo! the

fiddle strikes up a lively air, which makes the
simple folks laugh and weep and dance by turns.
Many fairy queens are beautiful to look upon,
but their beauty and virtue seldom go together.
Others, again, are ugly old hags, the servants
of the Evil One, of whom even Satan is
ashamed.

The latter class, according to Hindu superstition, is quickly discovered by the length of
the nose. It is said that a Hindu crone with
a long crooked nose is a *pretin* or fairy in disguise; and that the long nose was part of a
European fairy's stock-in-trade is familiar to the
annals of the poor in every country. Even a
versatile fairy named " Punch," who lived some
time after the Flood, was generally celebrated
for a very long nose, which was of great use
for " smelling out " new jokes and the blind
people who failed to see them.

There is a wonderful German fairy-tale, recorded, I believe, by Grimm, which describes
among other characters a fairy-being whose nose
projected right through a forest and sixty miles
beyond it. The story looks a little extravagant,
but has not given full details, or it would have
mentioned the American who ran a railway along
its length, and the Scotch financier who kept the
American and his concern on the go. Similarly,
wicked fairies of Celtic lore had big noses,
although they scarcely proved equal to those of

their German cousins. The Middle-Irish work called the *Geinelach Corca Laidhe* describes one of them as ugly and bald, uncouth and loathsome, her face very black, and her front tooth bigger than the square of a chess-board. "Her nose projected far in front, larger than the plough's cold share." It is thus apparent that whether the country be India, Germany, or Ireland, the nose of the wicked fairy stands out prominent, and betokens uncommon genius either for good or evil.

While superstition has undoubtedly much to do with the native love of exaggeration, example can prove that idiomatic expression is at its base. To show that he is highly elated, the Santal negro will say that his spirit has risen as high as a hill and his moustache has grown like ram's horns. When a Zulu wants a talkative neighbour to hold his tongue, he shuts him up by saying that his mouth is long and reaches over the fence. The use of hyperbole in such negro folktales may, in this way, be largely traced to those idioms which vividly express an exaggerated truth. It in nowise conceals the widespread belief that a person with a long nose is a wicked fairy in disguise, or connected somehow with great occult powers.

Among the Bantu, the nature of a disembodied spirit is defined in several ways. It is "life," and every one has given him a God-given spirit at the start. However, the Yaos hold that an infant has none until it is at least six days old. In proof whereof, they say, the custom of ancestors compels them to make it offerings and other tributes of respect should it die when six days old or more; while if it die before this, it is unlamented because without spirit. The spirit clinging to the body during lifetime is called the *lisoka;* when disembodied, it becomes purely *mulungu*, the corrupted word for "great" which is often used for "spirit," although properly an attribute of God, as is obvious from the full title in Zulu, *Unkulunkulu*, the "Almighty." It is this local misuse of terms that has resulted in the confusion of ideas, because when the natives say that a man after death returns to heaven and becomes "god" or *mulungu*, they really mean he becomes a *mulungu*, "spirit," but not *Mulungu* Himself.

Of other terms for spirits, they are at one in describing spiritual qualities and characteristics; and all convey the ideas of shadowiness, fear, greatness, goodness, evil, sacrifice, and worship. Each expresses a separate idea about the nature of the spirit, but most are emblematic of a nameless fear. It does not seem to be the spirits themselves who are feared so much as the power they have and evil they can do. Most spirits are bad, and those that are good-natured so seldom return to vex the living that they are said to go to a very distant country, which they never leave. They reach a land of beauty and love, and the world knows them no more. Thither bad spirits cannot come, being restrained from going by some law, force, or barrier of which man has no conception, and have perforce to cling to the world of the Fire-Spirit. A demon may thus hover over the earth and vex humanity for ages ; and neither time nor death can soften its malice nor temper its nature. It is to this belief that so many fairy-tales owe their being, which speak of fairy - changelings who, when exorcised, turned out to be fairies nine hundred years old and more.

The Old Gods of the Land.—Negro religion recognises a peculiar cult which is apart from the worship of God and the spirits of ancestors. It is a matter of history to show how the negroes, in the lands they came to occupy, exterminated or conquered the aborigines who preceded them. And well aware of the injury done them, they now seek to make atonement by pacifying their angry spirits.

Among the Kols the old pre-Kolarian population has disappeared, and yet as they worship to-day the ancient *bongako* or outraged spirits of the aborigines, the cult of the old gods of the land explains very simply why the Bengal negroes believe that the aborigines are still a power for good and evil, even though they have been a long time dead. As it is now five thousand years approximately since the Kols came into Bengal and seized the land and killed the people, it is ordinary reason to suppose that the spirits of these aborigines have reached that hoary age. In various parts of the Kol country are extensive ruins attributed to the preceding race. Those in the Manbhum district of the Santals, as at the ford of Barni Ghat, are said to have been the work of the mythical Jains. Some have monoliths erected to their memories, and others murdered in the "Good Old Times" are remembered by dolmens and cromlechs. Further than that the native traditions are silent, but many learned people in this and other countries have written large volumes fully explaining their use and origin. All these like sheep have gone astray.

To appease the *bongako* of those now more powerful after death, the Kols find it expedient to soothe them with prayers and sacrifices, especially in times of sickness and trouble. Most villages maintain a priest of the Naiyas, a semi-Hinduised caste of aborigines chosen for this particular cult. Of them it is explained that they are "employed to propitiate the aboriginal deities who are still supposed to occupy the place from which their original worshippers have been ousted."

From the cruel treatment meted out by the

Bantu to the races they vanquished or extirpated, and the subsequent remorse of the victors when, in turn, trials and troubles fell thick upon them, all which they ascribed to the angry gods of the land, arose the strange cult of appeasing a nameless class of spirits who are never worshipped among the ancestors. It is this same fear rather than respect that makes a conquering tribe refuse to desecrate a graveyard or touch the offerings of the dead. If war be declared between two villages, and one taken and destroyed, the vanquished flee to the bush, but return at night with offerings to the graves of ancestors, spending the night there in prayer to Mulungu and the ancestors for a better fortune. Next day the victors find big offerings of beer and flour at the graves, and know their enemies have come to them in the night. But rather than take such a welcome supply of food they would starve. They know that the sacrilege would lead to the revolt of the old gods of the land; and to avert any such dire misfortune Bantu custom demands the elevation of one of the conquered race into the ranks of the priesthood. He becomes the mediator who reconciles the old gods or spirits to the alien victors, and his chief duty is to pacify them and gain their support in the victors' behalf.

There is on record an historical example of how this strange cult arises. In the struggles

between the Yaos and Wanyassa the invaders
proved too much, and their final domination in
the land became a matter of time. Among the
latter the spirits of the chiefs had always been
the priests of Mulungu, or rather the inter-
mediaries between Him and their people; and
although to the Yaos the chiefs were but the old
gods of the land they could not be lightly ignored.
The last of them was Kangombe, who, seeing his
country lost for ever, and overcome with years
and weakness, retired to a cave in the lofty hill of
Sochi, whence he never came out. Some day he
will come forth to lead the Wanyassa to battle,
and for that reason the Yaos still hold him in
awe. When the rains fail and their crops begin
to wither they ask forgiveness of Kangombe;
and the more easily to convince him of their
earnestness the Yao chief always selects priests
from the subject Wanyassa who can claim kin-
ship with the magic chief of the mountain.
These are wont to supplicate him with the
prayer: *Ku Sochi kwa Kangomba ula jijisa*—
"O Kangombe of Mount Sochi, send us rain!"

It is thus made clear that the negro worship
of the spirits of aborigines, as it prevails to-day,
is not to be confused with the worship of ancestors.
It is demon-worship pure and simple, and is a
step in advance of Spiritualism, since it puts into
practice the belief that spirits live for ages,—in
other words, the immortality of the soul. It is

also clear that this wicked class of spirits keeps in touch with humanity for thousands of years. It is dangerous to incur their wrath, because they are vindictive; and especially do they hate to be disturbed in their old haunts by strangers. What they demand is worship, not love; and it is they alone who have ingrained into the negro those feelings of superstitious fear for which he is so constantly abused.

Spiritual Manifestation. — Wherever Spiritualism is known the same proofs are offered on its behalf. As this admits of no gainsaying, it is useless for any scientist to appear sceptical, and foolish to give the answer of agnostic and atheist. Millions of humanity are not so easily gulled by charlatans, nor so uncritical of fact and reason as to universally adopt spiritual beliefs on the sole authority of self-seeking mediums and clairvoyants. All that one need do, therefore, is to briefly glance at the negro's proofs of spirit-life, and the reader can compare them as he likes with his own knowledge of the subject.

The first and most direct proof of spirit-existence is held to be manifestations. A ghost may suddenly appear to a man, whose first thought, after he regains his senses, is to wish himself anywhere else. It prefers the dark to the light, the night to the day, and whenever it appears is of ill-omen, and never bodes any good. To make sure that they are awake the Kikuyu of British East Africa rub their eyelids with a piece of fat when they see a ghost, and they say it sometimes looks like a colobus monkey. In the morning they sacrifice a sheep to the troubled shade, hoping thereby to please it and avert coming misfortune.

Very seldom does a ghost show itself during the day, but stories are told of deceased friends passing people in the village or market-place. Spending an existence without definite form or substance, it need not even appear human. It may assume the shape of a lion, deer, cat, snake or other creature, according to the dictates of its fancy; and most likely it is this spiritualistic belief which gave rise to the numberless stories and legends about human mermaids, vampires, werewolves, and other figures of romance which adopted animal and human forms as they pleased.

Another proof is that animals can see ghosts when men fail to locate them. If they make sudden acquaintance with a ghost without proper introduction, animals dumbly protest by refusing to budge, tremble and sweat profusely, while showing every symptom of alarm and fear. Balaam's ass saw visions, and in this it was not exceptional. "True tales" have been told how a horse, shying at an apparition, threw its rider, and thereby caused the death which the spirit either desired or came to forewarn.

The Call of the Dead.—A common negro superstition about dogs is that they can see ghosts, and greet them with a mournful howl. In Central India this is explained by the fact that they see *Yama Dut*, the Lord of Death; and in many other parts of the country it is believed that the unusual howling of dogs and scream of kites betoken the approach of celestial beings who have come to take a departing soul to heaven. Or it marks the arrival of the Snake of Death, which is to snatch the souls of the dying; but among the Kols in particular it is rather the cunning jackal (*karaj*), "God's Watchman," which brings the last summons to the dying. Certainly most people associate its weird cry with death, and think when they hear it at midnight near a house that *Hudul Raj*, King of Hades, is hurrying to the house or village to gather in new victims to his fold.

The Call of the Dead is further illustrated in Zululand by a superstition remarkable for its popularity throughout the negro area. The *Batakati*, or witch-doctors who hunt up dead bodies, are wont to give them physic which at once brings them to life. By their power of magic they turn them into owls, cats, and other creatures of ill-omen; but before sending them on their missions of evil, the doctor cuts out the goblin's tongue so that it may tell no secrets, and burns a hole in the top of its head with a hot wire. Such is the native description of the *um-kōvu*, which is sent against an enemy or hostile kraal to bring misfortune and death. Whoever sees it dies on the spot; and whoever hears its wailing cry eats medicine to ward off the death that is very near him and his friends. In the silence of the night there steals an unspeakable dread over everyone when is heard the fateful call of *Maye! Maye!* (Alas! Alas!)

The *um-kōvu* of Zulu story and legend appears strangely similar to the dwarf-demon of Central India. He is said to be a funny-looking mannikin with a high-peaked cap, which renders the wearer invisible. He utters the shrill cry of *Miau! Miau!* and will tear to pieces any human being he meets. In Europe the malevolent troll can be recognised with ease. The night-raven of Scandian lore is a suicide who has been buried with a stake in his inside where three estates meet. It flies about crying *Bau! Bau!* and is ever ready to attack anyone it finds outside the house at night.[1] Its place in Celtic tradition is taken by a headless sort of Brollachan, Bauchan, or bogle, which can only utter an uncouth sound, which the Gaels have translated to mean "myself"—"Mi fhéin! Mi fhéin!"[2]

It is thus possible that, by observing the frequent connection between the unwonted howl-

---

[1] Craigie's *Scandinavian Folklore*, p. 334.
[2] Campbell's *Tales of the West Highlands*, vol. ii. p. 203.

ings of animals and a man's death, the negroes
have led themselves to believe that they are due
to supernatural agency, and that the animals are
frightened at seeing the deadly messengers of
Fate arrive. The spirits had something to do
with them, and, although no man can state with
certainty what amount of truth may lie in these
superstitions, their identity and prevalence in
Central India and Africa give them an antiquity
of some thousands of years, and justify humanity
in its fond belief that there is a something
behind them all which it is difficult to grasp or
explain. Superstition is often but the offspring
of ignorance added to sound reasoning and
acute observation.

Spiritual Telepathy. — Another proof is
Spirit-Thought. The habit of waiting on the
spirits to receive a message is of no modern
date. With the advance of education, of course,
customs are altered and improved, and there is a
natural tendency to move further from the stage
of the unsophisticated negro. Formerly, men
were content to sleep in temples, invoke the gods
there in dreams, and encourage their approaches
with presents of beer and flour. All that is
changed nowadays. Men and women go to
séances in semi-dark rooms, and clasp each other
affectionately in the gloom. When the lights are
low, the spirits of ancestors appear, and when the
mummery is ended the medium comforts the

departing brave with the spirits' usual message :
" Do not worry! all is well."

Most dreams are worth small notice, but those
which impress us take the nature of spirit-thoughts.
It is at night that the *ama-tongo*, or ancestors,
come to inspire people or warn them of the future,
and the dreams are their thoughts. The technical
Zulu term for a "dream-thought" or revelation
is *Ambulo*, a word whose original meaning is
explained by its Santal cognate *upel*, "to arise,
appear"—commonly said of a *bonga*; and that
dreaming and thinking have always been synonymous terms to the negroes from the beginning of
their history is proved beyond a doubt by the fact
that the negro word for "dream" is derived from
the verb "to think."

Further up country, the Angoni Zulus say
that in dreams they exchange thoughts with the
spirits, whom they call by a name which denotes
their habits of wandering. Moreover, the Yaos
and Wanyassa say they can even make the nightly
visitant reveal its presence, if, before going to
bed, they pour a little flour on the ground till it
forms a cone. By its appearance in the morning
they discover whether the spirit has touched it or
not. Food attracts the spirit at all times, because
it is a diet of worship.

Different from all ordinary spirits is a certain
class never seen of mortal man. They appear in
dreams only to witches and wizards, and are

even more bloodthirsty than they. Among such
are reckoned the *Hili, in-Canti* and *um-Kōvu*, all
of whom belong to the mysterious in Nature.
To them are attributed violent deaths such as
cannot be traced to human agency. *Angenena*,
"he was spirited away," is how the Santal
negroes explain the sudden disappearance of a
man. He may have gone to "shepherd the
alligators" under protest, but in any case he has
vanished. The Zulus believe that if anyone is
drowned, he is "called by the river." Should
he tumble into a deep pool and the fat little
Tokoloshe be there, he will not come out so
quickly. And if a shark or alligator devour a
man unknown to his friends, nobody pays a fine
for his violent death, as there is no tangible
evidence to suppose that he died.

On such occasions nothing can be done
except to offer a bloodless sacrifice to the river
or river-demon; and it is bloodless because it
is not for the ancestors. Nor are prayers made
on the deceased's behoof, as there is none to
tell whither he has gone. The custom amply
shows that the mysterious in Nature is not
worshipped, but that some demon-spirits, neither
human nor divine, are accorded a place outside
the worship of God and the ancestors.

Animals as Mediums.—As a fourth proof
in support of the existence of spirits and their
unquestionable interest in human welfare, there

is usually brought forward the subject of omens
and spirit-warnings. In this case, the personal
manifestation of the ghost never occurs, for its
message is delivered through the medium of
men and animals. To meet a funeral or a red-
haired man, or to stumble at the outset of an
undertaking, are evil auspices. Should a negro
hear, or think he hears, the voice of his dead
mother calling him by name, it is reckoned a
bad omen. No matter then how dearly he loved
her on earth, love gives way to abject terror of
the future, since he has an ineradicable belief
that the Call of the Dead is the forerunner of
misfortune. But if he hear himself called by his
mother several times, whom he knows is alive
among friends in a distant kraal, the omen to
him signifies that in a few days she will die—
probably from age or disease.

As a rule, however, spirits prefer to speak
through animals which are docile and more
easily controlled than men, and these become
the omens for men to read and learn. A few of
those peculiar to negroland may be mentioned
on account of their prevalence and popularity.
A black crow settling on a roof or flying across
a house, the croak of a raven, and the howl of
a dog at night, betoken death to an inmate. A
long list of other omens deals with minor ills
such as sickness, pain, injury, loss of wealth,
and various misfortunes; and the monitors of

these are chiefly the eagle, owl, cat, jackal, leopard, hyena, and snake. These are the servants of the *Mfiti*, "wizards," whom it is unsafe to meet or see in the dark. The witches and wizards ride on their backs at night in quest of dead men to eat, and the bark of the jackal calls them to the gory feast. They spend the night in fearful orgies, and should anyone see an unusual light or fire on a distant hill, he knows that their cooking-pot is steaming there with its fill of human flesh.

Misfortune of any kind is never too petty to be ignored by a spirit. Even a disappointment is forewarned; and this is done by means of a cat, baboon, rabbit, or snake. When one of these crosses a man's path, he knows that to proceed further in his undertaking is dangerous.

The Snake in Negro Lore.—Of reptiles the snake is at once the most loathsome and dreaded, and stands for all that is venomous and deadly. But while the symbol of death, it is also that of fertility, and held in great honour in India by numberless priests, charmers, and worshippers. The negroes have no form of snake-worship, and detest the reptile especially throughout the rainy season. As the Zulus explain, snakes are then so numerous that they must have dropped from the clouds. The common folks know where all the swarms of locusts come from, for they are driven from the

north by *u-Mabelemade*, Queen of the Long
Breasts ; but no man can tell where snakes come
from, or how their accursed brood is so ubiquitous
in the rainy season.

Human aversion to the snake has led to the
universal belief that a snake crossing one's path
is of ill-omen.   The Zulus hate it so much that
they will scarce mention it by name ; so a man
suffering from snake-bite will tell his friend that
he has been "pierced by a thorn," or "noosed by
the grass" (*uhilwe utshani*), and the friend takes
the hint, and asks no questions.   When one bears
another a grudge, he will exclaim, "Bone of a
snake pierce him whom you hate!" expressing
thereby the hearty curse that the rotten bones
of a dead snake will severely injure the bare
foot of his enemy should he unwittingly step
on them.

To meet a snake is a misfortune, and an
omen bad enough to stop business of any kind.
So much is this believed that the Angoni Zulus
have been known to delay a war because the
inauspicious sight of a snake crossing the path
of their army made the bravest quail before it.
Yet it is not the snake itself that is feared—it
is easily despatched—but rather the message it
bears to men.   The omen is an indirect warning
from the spirits, to ignore which would mean a
greater penalty than disappointment.   In this
way the snake gets into native folklore and idiom,

but it always personifies the evil in Nature. Zulu idiom adds frequent terseness to its expression by an appeal to the habits of the snake. As a symbol of deadly hate, it occurs in the phrase, *Ngingambekela nenyoka*, "I could make a snake for him"; the meaning being that a man, if he could, would put a snake in his neighbour's road, and thus disappoint his hopes and blast his prospects.   As a symbol of sickness, it is seen in the common phrase, *W'eqile umkondo wenyoka*, "He walked over a snake's track"—a Zulu circumlocution for "nettle-rash," it being supposed that sickness comes to anyone foolhardy enough to cross a snake's track, and the form it takes most often is nettle-rash.

Spirit-Control.—Such is a rapid survey of the great subject of Omens and Spirit-Warnings, usually dubbed superstition by those professing to be learned sceptics. Their number and universality alike proclaim their age and importance, and show that from the earliest ages humanity has found some truth in them. It is not the objects or creatures that are respected, but the messages they seem to convey while acting unconsciously under spirit-control. They are but the passive mediums whereby the spirits of ancestors declare their will; and this being matter of general belief, it has become an easy step in the process of reasoning to deduce from them that the spirits of the dead could assume the forms of animals when they chose.

Nevertheless, while millions of humanity believe in the spirituality of these countless omens, it remains indisputable that they form no part of Revealed Religion. However much they strengthen faith in spirit-being, they detract from the virtues of religion by appealing to the Unseen. And the results are sadly manifest to-day. The negro, having learned too much about Spiritualism, such as man was never intended to learn, has given all his mind and heart to the adoration of the saints or ancestors, and other classes of spirits in the unseen mansions of the other world, to the detriment of the worship of God and his own moral and intellectual improvement. More than anything else, Spiritualism has degraded the negro's best instincts, and taught him to go through life with fear and trembling. It has led him to feel that he is a secondary being in the hands of unseen forces, so that he cannot rise above himself; has stolen from his heart the ancient love and peace of God, and implanted in its stead a nameless fear that haunts his mind and dogs his footsteps to the grave. Spiritualism is the devil's religion, and the negroes know all about it.

With African doctrine, health means spiritual soundness and vigour. A healthy soul in a healthy body makes a healthy whole. This is the

Bantu negro's creed ; his chief end in life besides glorifying and enjoying himself ; and when he feels out of sorts, his body, mind, and spirit are equally affected. During sickness, the spirit leaves his heart and wanders at large, and to catch it the doctor is called in. First of all, a loud consultation is held about the fee, and then the devil or sickness that drove the soul away is discussed. A roaring trade is done by the doctor, whose aim it is to lure back the soul with mystic charms and poultices. Meanwhile, the patient keeps the peace as well as he can, observing with a sense of rising awe and fear the ingenious methods resorted to for his recovery. Like most negroes he will while away the time whistling for want of thought, or in serious mood ponder on the immortality of the soul, and his probable chances of a longer life. And just as the throb of an engine or aching tooth produce two different kinds of music, so likewise do the patient's woes and pains, and the doctor's driving away of evil spirits, together produce two different kinds of melody.

The same course of action is followed by the Santal doctors, their idea being that in sickness and deep sleep the spirits of men fly away from their bodies to hold communion with the ancestors. People have been known to go to sleep, and in the morning were found dead just because their spirits through the night had forgotten to come back, or else lost their way. For this reason, they are called after their wandering habits, *Horatenkoa Bongako*, "spirits of those who wander," the like idiom being familiar to the Bantu.

Spirit-Obsession.—The travail of the spirit is due to its restless energy. Seldom can it find peace and content; and although it be righteous and have both, its powers for energy and work are not in the least disturbed. The devils have plenty energy but no rest, and they for ever wander about seeking whom they may devour. Endowed with great spiritual strength, they can take possession of any weak soul until some stronger devil or devils cast them out, and in this wise the man's state is made worse than the first. It is to them that all the ills under the sun are traced, for devils are loathsome, and contact with them defiles the man, and brings him sickness and disease. In short, they obsess men by controlling or driving away their timid souls, and cause them temporary illness through loathsome infection.

When this happens, a man is said to be *possessed*, since he has lost his *self-possession*. He is no longer *himself* but *absent-minded*, and never talks unless *inspired*. If he take to writing, he does so *automatically*, and as if he was *not all there*. I maintain that *cacoëthes scribendi* is a disease of this nature, infectious and dangerous, sickening the dispirited reader till he is possessed with a spirit of revenge to injure the poor devil of an author.

Evil spirits possessing men are the cause of most troubles among the Santals, one of many complaints being *bonga khoda*, a painful finger-sore which affects the arm up to the shoulder. Some are voluptuous, preferring to take the forms of youths and maidens who visit homes, and lie with inmates of the opposite sex. Such liaison brings ill-health to man or woman, and the unlawful visits of the *bonga kora* and *bonga kuri* can only be stopped by the *Soka's* charms and spells. The *Soka* is the witch-doctor, and it may be of interest to observe that his name is etymologically identical with Zulu *um-Takati*.

A man acting in an unusual way is *bonga chapar*, "spirit-possessed." If he keep shaking his head, the people say he is a wag possessed with the monkey-spirit *Haru*. If he laugh too loud and long, the Laughing-Spirit *Landa Bonga* has caught him. If suddenly seized with a fit, he is possessed body and soul; and so, when people have convulsions, it is said of them, "They are inspired by the spirits." Often when the priest wants information about anything, he gets into communication with the spirits by repeating certain charms and incantations. Such an oracle is called *Chauraha*, and is expected to reveal everything. But oracles are the same all the

world over.   They do not open their mouths
save for a consideration.

Avenging and Protecting Genii.—African
negroes, on the whole, are an ignorant and care-
less lot; and because they are never at fault,
they attribute to wicked devils what results from
their own wilfulness and characteristic neglect of
any sanitary rules to preserve health.   Besides,
as the native explains his diseases to be an attack
of the Avenging Furies, he reasons that they are
punishments or divine dispensations sent either
by Mulungu or the spirits.   In either case, they
are due to spiritual anger; but there is this difference, that God's anger is sure and effective
without any form of obsession, whereas that of
the spirits is induced by obsession alone, and can
be prevented.   Diseases therefore come to be
regarded as so many devils (*pepo*), and the faith-
healer or Christian Scientist is the Devil-Doctor
(*mganga wa pepo*), whose duty it is to cure people
by driving out the devils wherewith they are
tormented.   This he does by lashing his patient,
biting his flesh, and suggesting that he has
caught the devil in his mouth; by exorcising the
demon and the laying on of hands.   Sometimes
food is offered to pacify the devil—not the patient
—especially if it be known that its body was
formerly denied burial.   A devil of this sort is
very malevolent, and like the house-haunting
ghosts is wont to make much ado about nothing.

On a higher plane is the Protecting Genius, which sometimes suggests to the doctor a specific cure. The functions of this class of spirits are as varied as their powers. They give good auspices, make journeys successful, avert famine and disease so far as they can, forewarn relatives of coming misfortune, but it does not appear that either good or bad spirits can forewarn death. They never haunt houses and make themselves a fright; and when they do come—as in the form of a harmless snake — they depart without causing any trouble or inconvenience.

Nor does their virtue and kindness rob them of valour, for they fight unceasingly with wicked spirits on behalf of their friends. When wise heads come to loggerheads and then proceed to break heads, their respective *Madhlozi* in the air above are believed to be similarly engaged twisting, fighting, biting, and screaming at each other. And when one of them succumbs or "softens," the man below, whose attendant it is, succumbs also. For this reason, the battle is lost to the *idhlozi* or guarding genius. The man himself is considered not at fault.

Thus is it that the negroes find work for the two classes of good and evil spirits of ancestors. Nor are they singular in their belief. According to mediæval Christianity, a slight adaptation is to be found in the belief that angels ever bright and fair hover above the average sinner. Even till nowadays, despite changes in creeds and politics, the belief keeps tenacious hold on the world. "Angels" of approved sterling worth are still much in demand; always a desideratum, always welcome.

Christian Science among the Negroes. —There can be no doubt that the negroes have come to understand the meaning of Christian Science. There is no pain, no evil, no sickness in this world. The negro is the picture of innocence. He never goes wrong. What afflictions he may have are spiritual, because disease, like death, is an unnatural state of the body resulting from spirit-obsession. It matters nothing if a man sat up all night with a toothache that made him call it the "hell o' a' diseases." The fault is not the tooth's so much as that of the wicked spirit who put a little worm at its root. So with evil. A man is good or bad according as the spirits make him.

Such is the Christian Science of the negroes, founded wholly on Spiritualism and not Revealed Religion. It is not without justification in their case, seeing that they know so much about spirit-existence that to disbelieve would seem to them the merest folly. But while it is only a branch of Spiritualism to them, it is superstition to us; and as the negroes plainly demonstrate, it has no part in religion proper. If with us to-day it professes to teach religion, it is because

8

the devil is going with the times, and likes to make religion fashionable without the need of piety.

Deformed Shapes of Devils.—A final word must be said about a curious superstition which is remarkable for its antiquity. Negroes are generally given to trace very uncommon physical deformities to spiritual causes, as has been already shown in the case of a Cæsar, Napoleon, or other genius gifted with a prominent nose. When a woman's eyebrows meet, it is proof that she is a witch devoted to cannibalism.

In the *Katha Sarit Sagara* there is a story told of an Indian demoness, described as of repulsive appearance on this account. "Her eyebrows met; she had dull eyes, a depressed flat nose, large cheeks, widely parted lips, projecting teeth, a long neck, pendulous breasts, a large belly, and broad expanded feet." A Lithuanian superstition holds that a witch, whose eyebrows meet, likes to eat human flesh; while in Norse Mythology the werewolf can easily be recognised by the meeting of his eyebrows above the nose.[1]

Long ago Strabo once came across this superstition when gathering material for the Indian section of his great geography. But he put on record as fact about the *Enotocoitæ* what was really nothing but fable. This people of Indian

---

[1] Thorpe's *Northern Mythology*, vol. ii. p. 69.

legend had "ears down to their feet, so that they could lie and sleep upon them, and so strong as to be able to pluck up trees, and to break the sinew string of a bow. . . . *Their heels are in front, and the instep and toe are turned backwards.* . . . They live near the sources of the Ganges, and are supported by the smell of dressed meat and the fragrance of fruits and flowers." The tradition that seems to be referred to by Strabo is probably one that was well known throughout the Ganges valley. It is met with to-day among the Santals and other Kol tribes, to whom the Ear-Sleepers of Strabo appear as mythical one-legged demons (*eka guria*), who are cannibals, fond of killing people and eating them.

The Testimony of Tradition.—In addition, Strabo mentions a story about a wonderful people called the One-Eyed (*Monommati*), of whom he says they had only "one eye and the ears of a dog, the eye placed in the middle of the forehead, their hair standing erect, and their breasts shaggy." Du Chaillu, the explorer, came across the same superstition in his African wanderings, and found it coupled with the tradition of a superhuman, one-eyed race. Among the Apingi was a legend to the effect that in the far interior lived a people called "*Sapadi, who have cloven feet like antelopes.*" . . . "Wherever I have been in Africa," continues Du Chaillu, "I have heard this legend; and the nation called Sapadi are always situated in much the same place—in Central Equatorial Africa. It is curious that wherever I have heard of this people they have had the same name, Sapadi. . . . Among the Commi many people believe that the whites who make the cloth which traders bring them are not like us, but a race with one eye, and that in the middle of the forehead." [1]

This negro superstition, first discovered by Strabo among the Kols of Bengal, and then by Du Chaillu and others among the Bantu, owes its origin to the belief in a class of supernatural beings who are neither human nor divine. But it is not confined to the negro regions alone, since it turns up unexpectedly among the Papuans of the Indian Archipelago, by whom it is explained to refer to the strange shape which a Snake-Spirit adopts when assuming or attempting to assume human form. " Snakes can assume human shape, male or female, for the purpose of tempting men and women, and to yield to whose seductions brings death. . .. *When in human form the elbows and knees are reversed, the elbows being in front and the knees behind.*" [2]

The Papuan idea gives the nearest possible meaning of this strange belief, and however mythical it appear, the fact that it is known

---

[1] *Equatorial Africa*, p. 340.
[2] *Journ. Anthrop. Inst.*, vol. x. p. 278.

to the Bantu and Kol negroes as well as the
Papuans is scientific proof of the most convincing
kind that it is of antediluvian date.   On what
truth it is based, humanity before the Flood could
best tell, but, coloured as it may be with human
fancy, it maintains undying popularity.   As there
is a personal God, there is also a personal Devil
—the Congo Fire-Spirit or Snake-Spirit—who
tempts the woman to sin.

**Satan the Snake-Spirit — a Personal
Devil.** — The Snake-Spirit in European lore
becomes the lame Vulcan or Devil, with cloven
feet and hoofs, and as such he invariably appears
in the wild legends of the Basques.   On account
of his feet, Satan is likened to a goat, and hence
this animal is believed to be the central figure at
all the open-air conventicles of the witches.   The
Evil One is shaped like a big black-bearded goat,
and seats himself on a peak of the Pyrenees·
There he holds his court, and rewards the witches
and wizards for the evils they have done to
righteous men.   Wherever, therefore, these meet-
ings are held, the place is called *Aquelarre*—
"pasture-land of the goat"—and every sensible
traveller gives a wide berth at night to all such
unhallowed spots.

The belief among the Basques of Britain in
no way differed, and, owing to the predominance
of Basque religion and superstition among the
Celts, it makes its début quite naturally in Celtic

tradition. Of course, because the language of the text happens to be old Irish or modern Gaelic, the circumstance does not make it "Celtic," for the Celts could not explain its meaning, even if misdirected sentiment solved its origin.

In the old Irish folktale of *Tochmarc Emire*, *Olldornai* (Bigfist), daughter of Donald, is described in a way that shows how the old Basque belief about the snake-spirit still lingered among the Irish. The charms of this legendary lass are described after the negro manner. "Her knees were large; her heels in front and her feet behind. Her form was uncanny (or awesome)."[1] The same epithet which I translate "uncanny" is applied, in Scottish Gaelic, to the figure of the Lady of Death, otherwise known as *Muileartach*, *Muireartach*, *Mulathadach*, or *Buileardach*—"the uncanny, hideous, and crooked spectre"—

"An Tarrach eitidh, athull crom."

Like the Cannibal Old Woman with the Big Tooth in Kaffir tales, the Muileartach is described in ballads as a woman with one eye, shaggy hair, and blue complexion, and her single tooth encumbered with splinters of human bones. She appears in company with a unique character, by name *Roc Mac Ciochair*, of whom it is written that he had but one leg, one hand

---

[1] *Batar morai a gluine; a sala reme; a traigthi ina diaid. Ba hetig a delb.*

protruding from his chest, and one eye in his forehead.

> " Bha aon chos fodha nach robb mall,
> Bha aon làmh as uchd nach clì,
> 'S aon suil air clar a chinn mhòir."

With the personal charms of Roc, who is recognised in Celtic lore to be a demon, or superhuman *Fuath*, are to be compared the Cyclops, the Fire-Spirit of the Congo, and *Chiuta* of Central Africa, who never had human shape since the beginning of the world, and who appears occasionally to men with but one eye in his head and one side to his body. Such Snake-Spirits are personal devils, above the order of the ancestors and the old " gods of the land." They never tempt humanity to sin, save to compass their ruin and death.

Negro Knowledge of the Occult.—From the foregoing facts and arguments it is not difficult to see that the negroes have arrived at a knowledge of the unseen from other sources than observation. The Kingdom of Heaven cometh not by observation. But, as that knowledge is descended from an antediluvian age, scientific criticism can merely prove its antiquity. Their own explanations are not always of value, when we know for certain they depend more upon tradition than reason. They have, however, proved, satisfactorily to themselves, that life is spirit and spirit cannot die ; and that it is spirit forming the character of man in such wise that he maintains his individuality to all eternity.

Death forces the spirit to its proper sphere, where it first discovers its real worth, power, and energy. Consequently it becomes an object of fear to men, rather than love, being reverenced for its power more than for the good it may do. It is human in its senses and emotions, and, if wicked, feels more acutely the pains and sorrows, diseases and sicknesses associated with a life on earth, because it is not sufficiently spiritual to rise above bodily impressions. Good spirits are at rest, living without discomforts, and so it is the wicked who afflict men with trouble and disease. They try to get rid of their eternal burdens.

Lastly, spirits are not a heterogeneous mass, but appear in grades or classes, divided by unknown barriers. There are the good and bad spirits of ancestors and the old gods of the land. These three grades never commingle, although they are human in origin and instinct. Above them are superhuman orders of true devils, who never took human shape since the creation of man, because it is beyond their power so to do. When they make the attempt they appear rather as a hideous travesty. Opposed to them, and more powerful, are the good angels and the protecting genii; and thus has the negro satisfied himself of a graded after-life dependent on the present, and has long since conceived that life is spirit which turns the power of death into hollow mockery.

Further than this they have not gone. Negroes do not believe in the resurrection, because that is a new doctrine to men, taught them first by Christ as God's latest commandment. The leading difference, therefore, between the Christian and negro forms of faith is made obvious. In the one, spirit is everything—the body counts for little and disappears at death. In the other, spirit and body are bound together, and, although for a brief period death must claim the latter, in the last day, when heaven and earth shall have passed away and all things are made new, the re-union between body and soul will be accomplished. But with the coming of a new order the old will be reversed. After death and the resurrection we shall see Christ as He is, and be like Him, unconscious of our physical bodies' existence, because too spiritual to observe and understand it ; whereas before death and the resurrection the reverse holds true. We are scarce conscious of spirit—many deny its being— and are too obsessed with the knowledge of bodily weaknesses and infirmities to attempt, by the power of spiritual faith, to do those miracles which Christ did with such apparent ease because he lived in the Spirit and by the Spirit. The closest possible comparison between Christian and negro religion thus reveals a radical substratum of thought and belief, common to both while they have yet sprung up independently. Both indicate in plainest language that life is spirit, and spirit primarily an emanation from God. It is apart from things physical which, indeed, it but animates for a time, and the sole difference is the belief in the divine resurrection of physical bodies —a belief which the Christian religion alone possesses, being centred in the resurrection of Christ, the Son of God, upon Whom the Christian faith is founded.

CHAPTER IV

THE WORSHIP OF ANCESTORS

" No hillside without its grave ; no valley without its shadow.'
—*Zulu Proverb.*

REVERENCE is a trait of negro character which
seldom springs from love and respect. It is
begotten of fear, and tempered by experience.
And it is from fear of the dead that the Worship
of Ancestors has arisen. The power of the
released spirits of men being generally recognised, the efforts made to appease them and
solicit their help and advice, have introduced a
new form of religion which has outrivalled the
simplicity of the ancient faith. It has also
obscured it with superstition and error; and
only its undue importance in native opinion can
justify the statements of so many travellers that
atheism or demonism is rampant among the tribes
of Darkest Africa. From slight acquaintance
with the negroes and a superficial analysis of
their beliefs, they have chosen to call their
spiritualistic beliefs by the name of religion,
ignorant that below negro volubility about the
spirits of ancestors there lies a stratum of pure

faith in God, which reticence conceals through
European irreverence towards every sort of negro
belief.

Gods of the Household.—No one is in-
vulnerable, say the Zulus; all things end below,
and it is right and proper that the dead be praised.
From this motive of respect to the ancestors it
becomes a public as well as private duty to honour
the dead. Among the Mundas and Santals they
are entitled to a daily cult, and the form it takes
is usually to drop on the ground a few grains
of rice before meals. Similarly, before drinking,
a little rice-beer is spilled as the ancestors' share;
and this, added to the previous offering, consti-
tutes the negro's "grace before meat." In no
sense is it thanks rendered to God—although
He is not forgotten—so much as a sacrifice to the
Ora bongako or "household gods," to let them
feel that they are not neglected even if death has
parted them from their earthly abodes.

A more formal way of making reverence due
is carried out directly a man dies. A few days
after death, is performed the elaborate ceremony
of *Umul-Ader*, the " Bringing in of the Shade."
It begins with a public procession to the grave,
where the nearest relative of the dead man calls
aloud to his shade: " We have come to call
thee back to the house; thou hast now lain long
enough in the chill and cold." The silent procession is then reformed, and wends its way back

to the house.   At intervals on the route two ploughshares are struck together—a very ancient custom with a symbolical meaning ; and after some other rites of lesser importance are gone through, the shade is finally installed as an *ora-bonga*, " house-spirit," to be daily worshipped by the family.   When it is desired to have evidence of the spirit's entrance, dust and ashes are sprinkled on the floor, and should they appear to be disturbed through the night the sign is considered favourable.   The spirit has returned to live among his people.

Abode of Ancestors.—Negro houses have usually a but and a ben, the latter being the Munda *ading*, "inner chamber," reserved for the bones of ancestors, which are kept in an urn.   The inner room is not a living-room ; and so the Bantu make the ben in the grave itself.   This is an advantage rather than otherwise, because, being a wandering people, the dead are least likely to be disturbed in their graves after the people have left the locality.

The Wadigo of Mombasa are wont to dig a grave six feet deep, making a chamber at the side to receive the corpse.   This sepulchral ben is closed with a screen of matting, and the grave is then filled in.   The use of the ben is also familiar to the Baganda.   The ghost of a dead king lives in the inner apartment of his house, while the outer is to receive strangers and the public generally. When anything is wanted of the king, the priest enters the inner sanctuary, smokes a pipe or two, and begins to rave like a maniac. His carefully chosen utterances are deemed prophetic, for people think him under spirit-control.

The use of the ben was well known to antiquity, and is a feature of ancient temples and tombs. The Pelasgian oracles of Delphi and Dodona reveal beyond a shadow of doubt that the inner sanctuary was the peculiar *habitat* of the spirit, where none might intrude save a special priest. Nor does the Temple at Jerusalem offer an exception. The Holy of Holies was the sacred *ading*, and in fact a survival from pre-Jewish times, because founded on a Canaanite site, and built after a Canaanite model. It was the abode of a spirit, and never entered unless on special occasions by the High Priest to consult the inmate. The existence of the Holy of Holies is, therefore, proof positive of a more human cult than the worship of Jehovah. With all due respect to the later Jewish reverence for the Sanctuary, one must not forget that its construction was more suited to the needs of a pre-existing cult of ancestors or the Baalim, and that its association with the Being of God is not primitive. As we shall find later, the negro's God lives in a Temple not made with hands, eternal in the heavens.

Memorials of the Dead.—A very popular but misleading proof of negro degradation is argued from the common worship of stocks and stones. This is no truer in their case than it is in that of Roman Catholics, who venerate the relics of saints, pictures, and images. It is not the objects themselves that are respected so much as their associations with the saints who have gone before. Only one reasonable objection may be urged against the Adoration of the Saints as against the Worship of Ancestors, and that is, not the absence of Gospel testimony in their favour, but that both are identical in aim and purpose, and, as the negroes better understand, are founded on Spiritualism and not Religion. It may not, of course, be easy to trace at first the evolution of the Adoration of Saints from the Worship of Ancestors, but in a later chapter it will be shown that common to both is the old negro ritual which rests purely on Spiritualism.

The stone or idol is a memorial to the dead and a visible reminder of mortality to the living. It is a way of pleasing the spirit, the memorial being a mark of attention if not reverence. But the spirit itself never takes up its abode in the stone ; and if it does, the superstition is local and of late growth, seeing that the worship of the spirit is primary, whereas that of the stone is secondary and modern.

In Central India, the custom of setting up a

stone is believed to give peace to the troubled spirit. Offerings of cocoa-nut and rice are made from time to time, and the stone is carefully tended for some years. Once a year, for three days in succession, a lamp is left burning at the head of the grave ; then relatives begin to relax their attentions until a visit from his spirit vexes one of them with sickness. Immediately the care of the ancestor's tomb is redoubled and his wants satisfied.

Circles of Ancestors.—Among indigenous tribes like the Yerrakollas, Vekkiliyans, or Nayadas of Malabar, the stones of ancestors are usually set up within the village boundaries. The enclosed spaces are called *mālē*, the stones being ranged in a circle, each of which represents an ancestor. These are often washed with water, though perhaps not with the same elaborate ceremonies which the Jains perform when they wash their statues with milk. The Indian's care of their grave-stones is thus seen to arise out of the Worship of Ancestors, and in every instance the tribute is paid to the spirit represented by a pillar in the Circle of Ancestors.

The Bantu negroes are likewise scrupulous in honouring the dead. When a man dies in Zulu-land, his grave is dug beneath a large stone which is not removed during the excavations. The relatives bury the body at break of day, and close up the grave with another large stone so as to disappoint whatever human and bestial prowlers are in search of corpses. It is supposed that the witch-doctor (*um-takati*) tries to learn the whereabouts of a new grave, his endeavour being to make powerful fetish from the remains. Hence the graves of chiefs are carefully guarded by attendants; but, as a chief's grave often holds much of his worldly gear, the care of his tomb is rather to keep off unlicensed grave-diggers who go fortune-hunting by the light of the moon.

In Uganda, spirits are propitiated by the care of tombs. When a man traces his sickness to a spirit he has neglected, and the doctor has exorcised it and made him well, he goes straightway to the spirit's grave, trims it afresh, makes offerings, and vows to keep it in better condition for the future. However, a negro's vow is as short as his temper, and after his next illness he is back again repairing the grave. At Lake Moere in Nyassaland, the idols of the people represent their deceased parents, and before them they make offerings of beer and flour, and sometimes light a fire for them to smoke beside.

The worship of stones and idols serves to remind the living of their duty to the dead. In its most literal sense, it is not idolatry, but a form of reverence or adoration of departed worth. And above all, be it noted, it has prevailed wherever the ancestors are worshipped. The great Circles of Ancestors to be found at Stone-

9

henge, or in North Africa or India, alike proclaim in silent majesty the ancient care of tombs conjoined to the Worship of Ancestors.

Building the Cairns.—In many parts of India, tombs are mere cairns or large mounds, which, owing to their size, are a picturesque feature in the landscape. The natives pass them on the right hand, and the general custom of adding a stone is responsible for their greatness. The Irulas of the Nilgherries, for instance, raise cairns to the memories of their ancestors. After a funeral is over, each mourner throws a pebble on the grave ; and so the size of the cairn attests thereby the social position and following of the deceased. This custom is to be met with as far north as Kurdistan, in which country the cairns are commonly built by the roadside. Every true believer is expected to add a stone to the heap by way of salute, and this rule having been observed for ages has caused the cairns, from the accumulation of countless pebbles, to present nowadays a most imposing appearance. In symbolical fashion it is observed by the Mussulmans, who bury their dead as conveniently near the road as they can, so that devout passers-by may offer up their prayers for the dead. Thus will old customs live on by adapting themselves to the changing times.

In the Bantu country cairns are built over the dead to keep off wild beasts. But there is a deeper meaning than this, which so many negro tribes have forgotten. In Zululand anything in the nature of a memorial is called *um-kumbulo*, from *kumbula*, "to remember"; while a cairn is *isi-vivane*,—reckoned usually a sort of lucky-heap. The same word among the Kaffirs denotes the artificial cairns often seen in their country, about which an African writer says that the Kaffir "repeats no words, but merely picks up a stone and throws it on the heap that good fortune may attend him;" while a lexicographer says that, when adding a stone, he repeats the formula, *Tixo ndicede*, "God help me!"[1] The latter opinion is upheld by another African writer, who thus explains: "Alongside the great footpath thoroughfares of the country are found, at intervals, cairns or heaps of small stones. Travellers, as they pass, cast a small stone on these, and with uncovered head, say, "*Ah sivivane*, or Cairn! grant us strength and prosperity!" The spirits of the chiefs certainly hear the prayer of their children when they observe the customs of their country. . . . The action is regarded in the light of devotion."[2] Similarly, the Bechuanas erect a cairn of stones over the graves of their chiefs, to whom they pay marked attention and respect by adding pebbles to the cairns.

[1] Theal's *Kaffir Folklore*, p. 21 ; Davis' *Kaffir Dict.*, s.v. isi-vivane.

[2] *Journ. Anthrop. Inst.*, vol. xx. p. 126.

The ancient custom of adding to the cairns of ancestors is but another way of honouring the dead, from whom they expect favours in return. It has certainly less appearance of idolatry than the care of the tombs and stones of ancestors; nevertheless, they are both alike in purpose, and form part of the negro faith in the Worship of Ancestors.

Potting the Dead.—The old negro race of Bengal seems to have made little or no attempt to preserve the body from decay. Doubtless, the skill and means were wanting, even although in countries neither civilised nor remote the method of preserving the body by smoking and drying had long been in general practice. And yet ignorance of the art of mummifying made no difference to the negro, since his beliefs in Spiritualism suggested to him the artificial need for maintaining, if not preserving, the bodies of the dead. As the spirit lived, it was supposed, by parity of reasoning, that the body required nourishment in death as in life; and accordingly provision was made to supply its wants. To refuse it made the spirit angry because it was hungry; and before its favour could be gained the relatives had to satisfy its crave for food by a present of grain, flour, beer, fowls, and other offerings.

The peculiar manner of the ancients in the disposal of their dead went a long way to encourage men's beliefs in spiritual wants. In India's prehistoric days the body was placed in a large urn, and the better to fit its concave sides, was doubled up into a crouching posture. As has been proved from discoveries of ancient burial-places near Salem, Tinnavelly, Nellore, and Malabar, the great earthenware urns, from one to six feet high, were made on purpose to hold the dead; but as some of the jars are too small to admit a corpse, although found to contain ornaments, fragments of iron and human bones, it is likely that the bodies were first cremated before the ashes were consigned to them.

Such a form of Urn-Burial has every appearance of antiquity, but it is one not primitive enough to be obselete. Many tribes, like the Koramas of Mysore, perform numerous ceremonies before the urn or grave-pot receives its occupant; but these once over, the spirit is thenceforth domiciled in the pot, receiving from time to time supplies of food and drink. Even where it has become usual to cremate the body, as among the Kols, Mundas, and Santals, the full significance of the ancient custom is not lost; and so, after the corpse is consumed by fire, the bones and ashes are carefully gathered into an earthen vessel, which finds a place in the Abode of Ancestors.

Bantu tribes never "pot" their dead as they

did of yore, but plant them in graves shaped oviform like the ancient urns, to fit which properly the corpses are doubled up. Nowadays the real urn is kept outside the grave, and, a hole being made in the bottom, food or drink offered to a spirit sinks through the ground to nourish the dead body below.

From the negro point of view, the primary use of the funeral-urn is to hold dead bodies or their ashes, and its secondary use to receive the food which the living owe the dead. Furthermore, the dead ancestor is allowed a resting-place among the living, being worshipped along with other relics of the saints or ancestors; but the less ancient mode, as followed by the Bantu negroes, exchanges the worship from the house to the grave, a proof of change in the habits of the people, whose houses and lands were held on insecure tenure because the inhabitants were forever migrating to pastures new. The peculiar worship of the household gods would thus seem to belong to a race with settled instincts, and it is interesting to find how, in this respect, negro custom and belief helped to mould European culture as regards the disposal of the dead.

In the south-east of Iberian Spain, for example, the sepulchral urns for containing the dead of a prehistoric age were found to be of oviform shape. The position of the skeletons inside made it certain that they had originally been put there in a crouching posture with the knees drawn up to the chin—a form of negro burial far from rare in British barrows.   No less than 1300 vaults were opened, and about 150 cists and urns brought to light.   But while urn-burial in ancient Spain was genuinely a negro custom, it was not confined to the west alone, for we find it flourishing throughout Greece during the Mycenean Age.   Centuries after the Pelasgian era had passed away, the cultured citizens of Athens believed that souls could be seen entering and emerging from huge vat-like urns, and understood the verb ἐγχυτρίζειν, as used by Aristophanes, in the sense of "to pot," the sinister meaning being an echo of the days when the dead were potted in urns.   It is thus proved that Potting the Dead always played a leading rôle in the worship of ancestors, of which, indeed, it seems to have been an integral part.   Beyond question, the negro custom gives practical illustration of the prime duty of the living to the dead, by according them their rightful place in the inner sanctuary, where they assume the status of household gods.

The Graves of Ancestors.—Since the spirit was reckoned to be human in its wants and sympathies, men supposed that the right way to please the spirits was to feed them with what the living enjoyed.   Zulu faith in this belief may be said to be typical of the negro.   When an angry spirit visits the kraal, hunger is the cause of its visitation ; and to appease it, a grand palaver is arranged. The fatted calf is killed, and all the prodigals for miles around invite themselves to the feast. Only the heart, however, is reserved for the spirit, and because children are curious and sceptical, it is hidden in a pot at the back of the house, where an old woman stands on guard to keep off prying hands and eyes. On other occasions, less expensive sacrifices are made, but almost invariably, whether in Zululand, Nyassaland, or Uganda, the clay-pots of the deceased are set up at the head of his grave to receive the presents of food which his friends and relatives may choose to give.

In ancient Europe, this negro custom of nourishing the dead by putting food and drink in the urns or grave-pots was very popular, and Archæology speaks forth with no uncertain voice. At Mycenæ and other parts of Greece have been unearthed altars of an archaic type, round and hollow in structure, with a hole in the bottom evidently meant to receive blood and offerings. In Etruria, as in Pelasgian Greece, these altars were apparently intended for the same use and purpose as the grave-pots of the Bantu. From them is evolved the ecclesiastical altar of to-day which has become the symbol of Christianity. But however much Christianity has raised the grave-pot to a state of dignity and repose, and worthily transferred it to more sacred uses, the fact remains indisputable that the altar is the survival of the grave-pot, which in turn belongs to the adoration of ancestors, and not the worship of God.

Further evidence of this can be adduced from the great Standing-Stones such as were used instead of grave-pots by many prehistoric nations. Large numbers of these cyclopean monuments are classed by archæologists into holed and cupped stones, although they have failed to see that the holes were meant by the builders to receive the offerings for the dead, whose ashes rested at the foot of the grave-stones.

The significance attaching to their origin may be judged from the opinions held by the direct descendants of the ancient builders of the Monuments. Standing-Stones among the Santals and Mundas are known as *Sasan-diriko*, and under these the bones of ancestors are laid to rest with great ceremony, after they have been removed from the Inner Chamber of the house. To possess a Standing-Stone in the Circle of Ancestors is the negro's proof of having an ancestor in the village, and is his sole means to claim village-rights and privileges. Hence arose the popular saying, *Sasan-diriko Mundakoa patá*, "The Standing-Stones are the Mundas' title-deeds." Elsewhere in India, if the story and purpose of these stones be forgotten, they are

assigned to the giants (*Pandus*) on account of
their size; but all have in common the holes and
cup-marks suggestive of ancestor-worship. In
most places, the holes are utilised as receptacles
for food and rice-beer which, being tabu to the
living, proclaim them as ancestral altars pure and
simple. That the negro Pelasgians of Greece
were familiar with this cyclopean kind of altar
is a matter of history; and the meaning of the
Grecian Holed Stone was, as explained in the
words of Pausanias, " to feed the spirits of heroes
with blood."

Fairy-Food.—The Food of the Dead is
sacrosanct, and tabu to the living. But to terrify
even the hunger-stricken from touching it, stories
were invented about the awful consequences in-
curred by breaking the tabu. The principal diets
of ancestors, in Kol estimate, consist of rice-beer,
rice, and fruits, and on special occasions the
blood of a fowl or goat. Among the Bantu, the
offerings largely reflect the social position of the
giver; and of this Uganda affords conclusive
proof, the poor being content with the sacrifice
of a small fowl, while the rich give food, beer,
cloth, firewood, fowls, goats, and bullocks. And
when a sick man recovers health, he is generally
persuaded by his doctor to pour beer on a friend's
grave, where he invokes the spirit with the
prayer, " Let him who is strong, drink and overcome." If the grave need repair, the task is

done with much ceremony, the dedication-service being concluded with food and beer, the latter of which the negro quaffs much more than the spirit.

To seek trouble is the surest way to find it; but if you meet it unexpectedly, all you have to do, say the Yaos, is to put white beans or flour at the graves, and ask the spirits to do better. In the Bondei country, funeral services entail sacrifice of a goat ere the corpse is borne to the grave; and the explanation is that the offering to the dead man allows him to pass over blood, by which he knows that a brother on earth is left to love him. Calico, flour, and beer are the usual offerings to the ancestors, but these are mostly given when someone is sick of spiritual interference. When this happens, the Zulus are wont to sacrifice a cow or bullock, and beseech the *ama-dhlozi* for mercy and forgiveness with the prayer, "O ye dwellers below, shades of our fathers, there is your cow; the same we offer. Now let this your sick one recover; let disease depart from him; the cow is already your own."[1] On other occasions, the sacrifice of cattle is made to invoke the spirits' favour before battle; to appease them when angry, and to satisfy the promptings of filial affection, because the dead are always trying to get into communion with the living, while the living want to rid themselves of the attentions of the dead.

[1] Grout's *Zululand*, p. 136.

No respectable negro ever plunders the graves or steals the food of the dead. It is a grave offence, which violates the most sacred traditions. Besides, to do so would be an insult to the village, apart from inducing the wrath of ancestors. That the belief is ancient admits of easy proof, for even the sin of the children of Israel was their eating the forbidden sacrifices of the dead. They were guilty of sacrilege, and the punishment that followed was traceable to the wrath of ancestors.

Superstition ever lends force to argument. Many stories and legends condemn the sacrilege, and boldly assert that whoever breaks the tabu will die ; and if, like the wizards, he goes in trance or deep sleep to Fairyland, he will never return to the living on account of his sin. The Zulu *Tale of the Resurrected Brother* amplifies this superstition. The resurrected brother who was lost and was found, was dead but came alive again, revisited his native kraal. There he told his friends how he had been in a fine country where everything surpassed the excellence of this world. He met a cousin of his in the other world, who had died a long while before, and who advised him to return to earth as soon as he could. Otherwise, said his cousin, he would be sure to meet someone who would offer him the food of the dead, and then he would be a spirit or *i-dhlozi* for ever.

Such a type of tale is known to the Papuans.

A Fijian folktale narrates how a woman once went to *Panoi*, or Hades. She had no difficulty in getting there, and saw many of the old familiar faces. Her friends were surprised to meet her, but did not notice that she was still in the flesh. She called on her brother, whom she found lying ill in a house—for he had just lately arrived, and was not yet reconciled to his new abode. Nevertheless, he was glad to see her so soon, and cautioned her to eat no food of the dead in the land of shades or else she would never return. By following his advice, she escaped to earth again to see the welcome light of day.

Legends to the same effect exist in New Zealand and Japan. When the Japanese hero Izanagi descends to Hades to persuade Izanani, his wife, to return to earth, the latter mournfully replies, "Alas! thou art too late. I have already eaten the food of this world."[1] Similar reference may be made in passing to European opinions about Fairy-Food. In Wales, Ireland, and the Isle of man, partaking of the food is believed to bar the soul's return to earth; and in Scottish lore, though people often enter the fairy-knolls and commune with the dead, they always come back to their friends, provided they have refused the food the fairies offer.

In Greek folklore, the tale of Persephone describes how Pluto carried off his bride to the

[1] *Journ. Anthrop. Inst.*, vol. vi. p. 57.

infernal regions, where he and his wife kept
Pandemonium. When Ceres sought Persephone,
and had appealed to Zeus for aid, Zeus told her
that her daughter could return to earth if she had
not tasted the food of the dead. Ceres took the
down-road to Hell for the sake of her daughter,
but found that she had eaten a pomegranate
plucked from Elysian fields, and thus her only
chance of return to the land of the living was
effectually cut off. Ascalaphus was the only one
to see her eat it, and he lived to regret the
rashness of his tongue. The goddess turned him
into an owl for telling the truth, and he hooted
long enough after that.

Lucian makes mention of the food of the dead
as tabu to the living at the Mysteries of Eleusis.
"Much wine was set out and the tables were full
of all the foods that are yielded by land and
sea, save only those that are prohibited in the
Mysteries. I mean the pomegranate and the
apple, and domestic fowls and eggs and red sea-
mullet, and black-tail and crayfish and shark."
At the *Chytroi* or Pot-Feast of the Athenians the
same tabu was religiously observed. The feast
was given over wholly to the dead, and was not
to be touched by the living. "It was dead men's
food," says a writer, "a supper for souls." From
this it becomes clear that the Eleusian Mysteries
was nothing but the Feast of Ancestors, given
over to the worship of spirits and the com-

memoration of the dead.   They taught men
to cultivate reverence towards ancestors, and
remember them at the Festival of the Recollection
of the Dead.

Hearth-Worship.—The first altars of men
were shown to be holed grave-pots or Standing-
Stones which received the food of the dead.
They were inviolable for what they represented,
and their careful preservation was a tribute to
the memory of the dead.   This is made further
clear from the relics of the ancient Hearth-
Worship devoted to the ancestors.

When a Brahman dies, custom enforces a
rigorous mourning for ten days.   The body is
burnt, and on the third day his friends and
relatives assemble at the burning-ground ; and
after collecting the bones, a bank of earth is
thrown up, and three stones set in position on
the mound.   One stone goes by the name of the
dead Brahman ; another by that of *Yama*, Lord
of the Dead ; and the third by *Rudra*, Causer of
tears.   These are bedecked with flowers and
garlands, and a sacrifice offered them amid much
weeping and groaning.   The Yanadis, a Telugu
forest-tribe, always set up three stones in the
form of a triangle at the southern or head end
of the grave.   In the space formed by the
triangle is placed a pot of water, and a hole
being bored in the pot, the water trickles through
to the head of the corpse.   Self-purification by

bathing and anointing the body concludes the burial service.

Among the wild tribes of Khondistan the three stones are held sacred. Together they are meant to represent the village idol *Zacari Penu*, and near them was sacrificed in the olden time the human victim or *Meriah*. Once a year a circuit was made round the marches, and the May Queen was borne along in the procession. On returning to the post set up near the three stones, the priest sacrificed a hog, and then the Meriah was slaughtered to ensure fertile crops. Apart from the Meriah, who was offered to appease the spirits with blood, the three stones hark back to the old ancestor-worship. This is clear enough as regards the Mundas and Santals, for the technical term *uthulak* signifies the rude fire-place of three stones, on the top of which the cooking-pot is customarily laid.

There is a similar superstition in Africa about the hearth-stones. The Kavirondo keep four stones in the form of a square, and plant in the centre a fig-tree, which is situated to the west of the village. This is the altar where the victims are sacrificed, the stones receiving the blood. Tradition says that they have been brought by the ancestors from a hill called Sangaro. The altar-stones of the Awawanga have likewise been handed down from generation to generation ; and their antiquity is such that nothing is known of their history, save that they are a sacred heritage to be carried about whithersoever the villagers migrate.

At the rain-festivals of the Bechuanas custom holds that, to obtain the favour of ancestors, the house must be redd up and purified at least once a year. This lends a religious atmosphere to a spring-cleaning. Each fireplace, which is built of three stones, has to be renewed; and the stones, now unclean, have to be changed or purified by the witch-doctor. The fire is extinguished, and the old stones are collected in a heap outside the kraal. The doctor thereafter goes round the houses with charmed torches, and relights each fire from the purified source.

Purification of the Dead.—In this way the ceremonial cleansing of the three hearth-stones is seen to be a relic of ancestor-worship; and the purifying of the hearth means indirectly the purification of the dead. The idol of three stones in the centre of negro villages is always the visible mark of an ancestral cult; and the lavish care expended on them manifests the public anxiety about the ancestors, while the ceremonial which surrounds their annual purification shows also that the worship is not intended for the stones, but for the living spirit-beings of which they are the memorials.

Another Bechuana custom, closely allied to

10

the foregoing, is the lighting of sacred fires.
Most frequently these are lit on the summits
of lofty hills by the priests, and in the native
mind are associated with magic and the spirits
of the dead. The custom is further explained
by tribes in the interior, who say that the
lighting of the fires on the hilltops by the
priests is connected with the purifying of
ancestors. Hence the sacred fires are kindled
by two charmed sticks, called by some " husband
and wife," the use of these being tabu to everyone save the chief and witch-doctor. The
manner of kindling fires on summits was also
known in ancient times to the negroes of
Canaan, and so to the Hebrews those fires
became synonymous with heathenism and idolatry.

The kindling of the fire at the tomb or on
the hilltop was a purification ceremony. When
the Atonga want to sanctify themselves after a
funeral the gravedigger lights a torch from the
dead man's hut and then jumps over it. The
rest follow him, and are purified by this means.
So in Zulu, from the verb *linga* (Santali—*lega*),
" to test, attempt, perform magic," we get the
noun *um-lingo*, a magical performance during
which a flaring torch is used for the purpose
of cleansing or curing.

In the classic world the torch played its part
in funeral ceremonies.

In the tale of Ceres seeking her lost daughter, Persephone, in the Underworld, and in the Eleusinian Mysteries, the torch was a necessary symbol. Nor was this prominence given to it in the Mysteries so singular. The tribes of Bengal and Assam hold a general feast annually for the purpose of laying to rest the ghosts of all who died within the year. It is held in the cold weather, immediately after the crops have been gathered in, and a period of gaiety ensues. A procession is formed outside the village, while inside the women bewail the dead over their graves. Two torches are placed on each grave, and as the procession files past the one torch is quenched with water and the other flung behind the house. The custom is not unknown to the Santals and Mundas, by whom a procession to the river Damuda is made once a year in memory of their forefathers and the purifying of the dead. The whole ritual, bound up with hearth-worship and the annual festival to celebrate the purification of ancestors, is further rendered important from the ceremony of the recollection of the dead.

Washing the Bones of Ancestors.—In Assam the harvest festival is followed by the remembrance of ancestors; and in Burmah the Tipperahs do the same at the harvest thanksgiving which takes place in November. As the dead are usually cremated at the riverside, the

annual mourning is held by the banks of the
sacred river. The Nagas of Assam devote part
of the month of December to the worship of
those who died in the preceding year. It is
believed that, on a particular night of the year,
the ghosts of ancestors may be seen passing
over the hills, driving slain men and stolen
cattle before them. The primitive Todas
cremate their dead, but keep a lock of hair
and portions of the half-burnt skull in a piece
of cloth. These are carefully preserved till the
day of *bara kedu*, "great festival-burning," which
is celebrated once a year, and serves as the
national Recollection of the Dead among them.

The annual ceremony of disinterring the
dead, and cleaning and washing the bones
before they are finally laid to rest beneath the
great monoliths and stone-circles, is familiar to
most of the aboriginal tribes of India. It has
been found among the Agariyas and other
primitive races in Central India, and among
Kols, Bhotiyas, and others away to the east.
In curtailed form the rite is known to the
Hindus as *Asthi-sanchaya*, "bone collecting
ceremony," the survival of a custom belonging
to the worship of ancestors.

In the mountains inhabited by the Mala
Arayans of Travancore there are many tumuli
and cairns in which the dead are entombed.
These graves or cairns are never opened till

the anniversary festival of Bone Collecting is held. The Savar Kols of Ganjam burn their dead and bury the ashes. Funeral feasts are held on the day after death, or at most a month after it, and on the anniversary of the Recollection the relatives dance round the spot where the body was burnt and set up a monolith near the village to the deceased's memory. This custom is observed by other Kol tribes like the Hos, Mundas, and Santals. The annual Recollection of the Dead is locally known as *Jang Topa*, or "Bone Burial," when the graves are opened and the bones taken out and washed before being interred, amid great ceremony and pomp, beneath the huge Standing-Stones near the village. During this festival the stones are decorated with flowers and anointed with oil in honour of the ancestors.

In lesser degree, the ancient Kol custom is observed in Africa. But among the Bantu it is unusual to burn the dead, and a sacrilege to open the grave; for which cogent reasons the old habit of opening the tombs and purifying the dead has completely fallen into disuse. In other ways they show that they do not forget the dead; and especially is this noticeable after harvest, when high festival is held. In the season of first-fruits, the ancestors are duly remembered and publicly honoured. The same is true of the Yaos, who reserve the season's first-fruits of the new crops of green maize, beans, pumpkins, peas, and other cereals, for the exclusive needs of the dead. The annual ceremony is technically known as *kulomba mulungu*, "to worship the spirits." The Wetumba, Wagogo, Warabai, and Baganda, observe the same rite annually; and to keep people from touching the food of the dead, many stories are told, especially to children, about the fatal consequences which will happen to anyone so rash as to eat the first-fruits. People have been known to burst and die, and others have eaten and swelled so much that nobody could recognise them.

Feast of First-Fruits.—The feast of first-fruits among the Zulus is called *Ukwechwana*. No one is allowed to eat of the first-fruits till the king has given permission. It is he who opens the New Year, and the feast continues for several days. On the last day, members of the royal kraal form a circle, which the king enters. He proceeds to leap and dance, singing the while of his glory and renown; and finally breaks open a green calabash before the assembled company. This signifies to all that he has opened the New Year, and allows the people to taste of the season's fruits.

At this time a very strange custom is observed. The warriors have to catch and kill a bull, but no rope or weapon of any kind is allowed them. Sometimes accidents occur, but if anyone gets horned by the bull, his death is attributed to his lack of agility. After the bull is killed, the doctor opens it to extract the gall, which he mingles with other medicines, and gives to the king and people to drink.

The bull at the annual festival is, in reality, an offering to the spirits, and affords another illustration of the remembrance of ancestors at this season of the year. But the Zulus are not alone in their manner of disposing of the bull. Of old, the Etruscans and Pelasgians sacrificed bulls very frequently to the ancestors, but the custom of the Zulus was best known to Greece. As recorded by Strabo, there was held in Ionia, once every year, a festival at Acharaca closely resembling the *Ukwechwana*. During its celebration, the young men and warriors, naked and anointed with oil, used to carry off a bull by stealth at midnight. They hurried away with it to a cave, where it was let loose, and, soon after, the bull would expire through the sulphurous fumes and vapour issuing from the ground. Such was the manner in which Pelasgian youths offered the bull to the spirits of ancestors.

The Night of the Dead.—In other parts of Europe there survive many customs and beliefs, which prove beyond shadow of doubt that the worship of ancestors was formerly

familiar to the different nations.   Among the
Slavs of Russia there still exists the custom
of *Pominatelnui Ponyedelnik*, or " Recollection
Monday"; because people on the Monday after
Easter remember their deceased parents.   In
the morning they crowd to the cemeteries, and,
after attending divine service in the various
kiosks, go and enjoy a meal over the graves
of their departed kinsmen.   This is done to
remember and honour the friends who are not
lost but gone before, but whom they are in no
hurry to join.

The Basques have a superstition that when
the *Arguiduna*, or Will-o'-the-Wisp, appears on
All Saints' Eve, the graves are opened, the
corpses show their fleshless faces, and grin as
they throw back and forward this nocturnal
firefly.   It is the sport of the dead during the
first hours of the second of November, when
the Roman Catholic church commemorates the
departed dead.   The superstition is interesting
as showing the ancient belief that the graves
were opened after the season of first-fruits, and
also because the Roman Church still preserves.
in its ritual the old beliefs and customs relating
to the worship of ancestors.   The festival of
All Hallows or Hallowe'en is therefore nothing more than a survival of the days in
Europe when the tombs were opened and the
bones of the dead taken out and washed.   And

it is far from improbable that the superstitions about Purgatory owe their being and popularity to the ancient ritual and ceremony regarding the Purification of the Dead.

The Worship of Ancestors, so prevalent all over the negro area, is founded on Spiritualism rather than Revealed Religion, and for that reason obtains an importance and popularity which it does not deserve. It is founded on fear of the spirits, and not filial love towards parents. Consequently, such form of worship tends to degrade the negro intellect, and elevates neither character nor morals. But at least, after all is said and done, it cannot be denied that if the negro has gone to a logical extreme in his beliefs about an other world, he has erred from having too deep-rooted a belief in spiritual life and energy. Death to him seems a short-lived nightmare, which flies away before the opening dawn of eternity. At best, to the negro it means a mere transition of human life from a lower to a higher and better sphere of existence—

> "——'Tis Death that feeds on men,
> And Death once dead, there's no more dying then."

CHAPTER V

" Heaven is not reached at a single bound,
But we build the ladder by which we rise
From the lowly earth to the vaulted skies,
And we mount to the summit one by one."

Ritual and Religion.—The differences between negro ritual and religion are perhaps nowhere more felt than in the subject which deals with native beliefs touching the social aspect of the Unseen. The negroes—or rather their Indian forebears of five millenniums ago—were so far advanced in spiritual lore that they knew how to distinguish the several classes of spirits or spirit-grades, morally divided into the two distinct orders of good and evil, but socially into various degrees of spirits, human, demonistic, and divine. There is, of course, no present hope of determining the source of that knowledge, whether it be derived anciently from Revealed Religion or human superstition. But this at least is certain : as upheld by Spiritualism, the negro beliefs are founded on aery facts, and these in turn, being common to the negroes of Bengal and Africa, prove on the historical side that they are of antediluvian date, and their genesis is to be traced therefore to those ancient civilisations of the world which dissolved at the time of the Flood.

It is not to be inferred from this that the negro has been bettered by his greater spiritual knowledge. Far otherwise. It has taught him the eternity of life, but not the value of faith, righteousness, and the need for repentance and good works; and has failed to help him to lead a better life or convince him of sin in the present. When he dies his goods are oft interréd with his bones, but so long as he dies of old age he has no fear of death, since he has no judgment-bar to face. He merely passes by natural transition into the beyond, where he takes his place according as his earthly manner of life has fitted him. Existence to him is infinite. Our present shapes our destiny, and in the spiritual condition we leave the world, in such guise we find ourselves in eternity.

Social Aspect of the Unseen.—If the old negro ritual of Europe be compared with that of the modern system of spirit classification among the negroes, it will be found that the latter is probably not identical with that of five thousand years ago. The grades recognised to-day, however, may be supposed to include two grades of ancestors, good and bad; the old gods of the land, good and bad; demon-spirits in Nature,

flung them down. The one who fell on a hill became a *buru-bougu*, and others whose lines fell in unpleasant places became deep-water demons (*ise bougu*), field demons (*noya bougu*), wood demons (*nesudzi bougu*), forest demons (*mo bougu*), well demons (*dauki bougu*), and river demons (*ila bougu*).

Spirits as Burning Lights.—Spirits are often recognised by their lights, the varying intensity of which reveals their rank. Of this the Basques offer a striking instance. They believe that good spirits are enveloped in a white light, the purity and brightness of the shining spirit according with its celestial rank. On the other hand, spirits that love the darkness appear bluish to the sight, and in their case also differences of degree are recognised by the luminosity of the bad bluish lights. These are chary of approaching the white and shining lights, because they fear the burning spirits of the good; and when they come to trouble men —possibly with the "blues"—they can only be put to flight by prayers for aid and protection.

According to the negroes, earthly society with its ascending and descending ranks or grades is perpetuated in the next world. When a Zulu king dies, he is surrounded by his wives and slaves, and buried in a lonely wood. There he is said to live in state among his people. Below him in rank come the tribal chiefs, village-

whose proper functions are imperfectly understood—such as the *um-kōvu*, *hili*, *in-canti*, and
lozikazana (a familiar spirit of the sorcerers which
whistles rather than talks); archdemons proper,
such as the Devil, Fire-Spirit, and Snake-Spirits;
guardian spirits or angels; and above them archangels, corresponding to the opposite rank of
archdemons.   Such are, approximately, the
different social grades in the Unseen, about
nine in all, having at the head the Person of
Jehovah, whose upper sphere is perfection
absolute.

Little is known as to how demons reached
the earth, but negro traditions, on what authority
it is impossible to say, support the truth of
Christ's statement that the Archfiend *Vulcan*, or
Chiuta the Fire-Spirit, fell as lightning from
heaven, and brought about the Fall of man.   It
was he who tempted woman to sin in order to
ruin her posterity, body and soul.

The Kol tradition about the creation of
demons is worth passing notice.   In the beginning, runs the Munda legend, God created the
earth and the *bongas*, and ages afterwards man
was created.   Then He left it through the
wickedness and persecution of men, and was
ascending to heaven when the *bongas* wanted to
go too.   They clung to Singbonga with all their
might, but as He would not have them in
heaven, He seized them by their top-knots and

flung them down. The one who fell on a hill became a *buru-bonga*, and others whose lines fell in unpleasant places became deep-water demons (*ikir bonga*), field demons (*nage bonga*), wood demons (*desauli bonga*), forest demons (*bir bonga*), well demons (*daddi bonga*), tank demons (*pakri bonga*), and river demons (*da bonga*).

Spirits as Burning Lights.—Spirits are often recognised by their lights, the varying intensity of which reveals their rank. Of this the Basques offer a striking instance. They believe that good spirits are enveloped in a white light, the purity and brightness of the shining spirit according with its celestial rank. On the other hand, spirits that love the darkness appear bluish to the sight, and in their case also differences of degree are recognised by the luminosity of the bad bluish lights. These are chary of approaching the white and shining lights, because they fear the burning spirits of the good; and when they come to trouble men —possibly with the "blues"—they can only be put to flight by prayers for aid and protection.

According to the negroes, earthly society with its ascending and descending ranks or grades is perpetuated in the next world. When a Zulu king dies, he is surrounded by his wives and slaves, and buried in a lonely wood. There he is said to live in state among his people. Below him in rank come the tribal chiefs, village-headmen, the professional classes, the genteel rich, the poor, and the serfs. Death removes no disabilities from any of these, nor makes people co-equal in power. Spirit-rank is therefore seen to be determined by social position rather than by spiritual wealth, and, in a somewhat opposite sense, it is proved what Christianity teaches: that we should store up for ourselves treasures in heaven by adding to our spiritual riches here below.

From all this it is easy to observe a striking difference between the Christian and negro faiths. In the one, the Gospel is preached to the poor rather than the rich; and humility and righteousness take precedence of wealth and social status. In the other, the exact opposite holds true because it is the doctrine of men.

The Nine Grades of Heaven.—But if the negroes love position and power rather than knowledge and virtue, they are by no means exceptional. In the religions of Greece and Italy, degrees of spirits were generally favoured. Over all the Creator Zeus reigned supreme, and after him followed the various ranks of spirits, gods, and heroes of the classic world. Very likely these degrees resembled those among men, as assuredly appears from the case of Etruria. Here there was a well-established monarchy and hierarchy, and the grades included king, chiefs, priests, the professional classes, the commons, and public serfs.

The number of these classes or ranks of men is briefly alluded to by Plutarch, who says that the Etruscans believed in eight different classes of men, and that a ninth was yet to come. Speaking of the prodigies which occurred during the Civil War between Marius and Sulla, he says: "One day when the sky was serene and clear, there was heard in it the sound of a trumpet, so loud, shrill, and mournful, that it affrighted and astonished the world. The Tuscan sages said it portended a new life and manners; and that heaven had allotted each its time which was limited by the circuit of the great year."

The Basques of Britain, who have left their impress on Celtic thought and tradition, also believed that there were nine grades in the other world. The ancient Irish law-tract of the *Crith Gablach* mentions only seven grades of the people, and this is explained to be proper, since the seven grades in the church should be the same in the people. But more often, in old and middle Irish texts where the celestial grades find notice, the stated number is nine; and the stock phrase in general use is *nai-n grad nime*, "the nine grades of heaven." In a tenth century poem on the *Day of Judgment*, in the *Calendar of Oengus*, in the *Aislinge Meic Conglinne*, and other compilations ancient and mediæval, the nine ranks of celestial spirits are alluded to so frequently as to put beyond doubt the popular belief in their existence.

By some it has been supposed that the idea of these ranks was taken from Dionysius the Areopagite, who explained them to mean: Thrones, Seraphim, Cherubim, Dominions, Authorities, Powers, Principalities, Archangels, and Angels. But this is a useless theory about abstract terms, and is of no value whatever, because the Druidic conception of the nine ranks is older than Dionysius, and belongs peculiarly to negro ritual.

The Devil imitates the powers of heaven without copying its virtues. He is not religious— probably never was—and yet if Indian tradition is to be believed, he religiously supports a family of nine sons.[1] In a tale from the Congo, it is the Queen of the Fairies who has a quiverful of nine boys. She married an earthly husband named Buite, a fisherman, whom she bade never to show her any of his fish-heads. Buite once forgot the fairy's tabu; and at this his enraged wife fled into the fairyhills of Congoland with her nine boys and was seen no more. Buite was reduced to poverty, and left to lament by himself the homely annals of the poor.

In British folklore, fairies are often found to

[1] *Indian Antiquary*, vol. xxix. p. 403.

be in nine companies or companies of nine. The legendary Merlin of Wales was attended by nine companions—*naw beird cylfeird,—cylfeird* being the Irish *culbard*, one of the nine bardic grades; and the same religious meaning is to be seen in the Gaelic appeal to the nine angels for protection—*naoi aingeal fionn.* "May the cross of the nine angels be over me," is the Gaelic formula—*Biodh crois nan naoi aingeal tharam sios.* That the Devil had nine sons is stated in the treatise on the *Life of Moling.*[1] He had a household of nine (*nonbhar muintire*), black, ugly, and unshapely, and to none on earth gave they sanctuary. Thus the Irish and Indian traditions agree on the same point because they draw their facts from the same ritual.

The spiritual significance about the number nine derives its importance from the belief in nine grades of spirits in the Unseen. Social inequality was intensified rather than otherwise; perhaps may have reflected the different grades recognised on earth, but this is scarce likely, as the modern spirit-classes of the negroes are reckoned after a moral standpoint which attaches small importance to claims of wealth.

Doctrine of the Many Mansions.—By force of reason the belief in spirituality and the nine celestial ranks lends itself to another, which supposes that the Land of Shadows is divided

---

[1] *Revue Celtique*, vol. xxvii. p. 269.

like these much of the native asceticism has
arisen, for many people imagine that by sub-
jecting the body to privation on earth the rank
in the after-life is elevated, and made the easier
to bear. In short, as regards the [...] religion,
asceticism illustrates the vaguer idea of [earning]
one's bliss in order to ensure a [...] reward
in heaven.

Among the [...] the doctrine of the Many
Mansions has almost vanished, yet tradition
still points to the fact that heaven is of itself
an indefinite [...]. There are several heavens.
While the supreme God of the race resides in
the sun—it is supposed to—His jurisdiction
extends to the "four winds and the four corners
of the world." To these fall to be added those
of tradition, *[...]*, *[...]* or *[...] [...]*,
and *[...]* or Hell, the last-named being probably derived from Hindu philosophy.

A belief, however, in some kind of Hades
manifested itself, as among the Bantu. The
Angoni Zulus speak of it as a state of being
and not as a locality, and it is there where
disembodied spirits go. Sometimes women go
mumming about the countryside, calling themselves "wives of Hades." They are smeared
with white clay and dressed up very fantastic-
ally, and, as they can turn themselves into lions
and other wild beasts the better to avenge their
fancied wrongs and dislikes, every one holds

into several stages of existence suited to the different ranks. Such a logical step may have led the negroes to conceive the doctrine of the Many Mansions, although this is far from certain.

Among the Gonds the tradition of the Many Mansions of heaven lingers in popular song. "In the ravines of twelve hills, in the glens of seven hills, is Lingawan, Mount of Heaven." In Hindu mythology the Golden City of the gods is said to have nine gates; and Paradise to be a silver bell with nine precious stones surrounding a square of four quarters. In the Chingleput district the aboriginal tribe of the Paraiyans believes that the dead have to traverse many strange regions before they arrive at the abode of the blest. They address the deceased in these words: "I gave you calves and money; enter the abode of Siva (*kailasam*); find your way to the Otherworld (*paralokam*). I gave you milk and fruit; go to the World of the Dead. I gave you gingelly and milk; enter the abode of the god of death (*yamalokam*)." The Nagas of the Himalayas think that if they lead good and worthy lives on earth, and abstain from all coarse food and flesh, their spirits at death will fly into the better regions of heaven and become stars. Otherwise, their bodies may have to pass through seven stages of spirit-life, becoming finally changed to bees. From beliefs

like these much of the native asceticism has
arisen, for many people imagine that by sub-
jecting the body to privation on earth the rank
in the after-life is elevated, and made the easier
to bear. In short, as regards the old religion,
asceticism illustrates the negro idea of bearing
one's cross in order to ensure a meet reward
in heaven.

Among the Kols the doctrine of the Many
Mansions has almost vanished, yet tradition
still points to the fact that heaven is of itself
an indefinite term. There are several heavens.
While the supreme God of the race resides in
the sun — or is supposed to — His jurisdiction
extends to the "four worlds and the four corners
of the world." To these fall to be added those
of tradition, *Hudul*, *Huripuri* or *Hihiri Pipiri*,
and *Ihkuur* or Hell, the last-named being probably derived from Hindu philosophy.

A belief, however, in some kind of Hades
manifested itself, as among the Bantu. The
Angoni Zulus speak of it as a state of being
and not as a locality, and it is there where
disembodied spirits go. Sometimes women go
mumming about the countryside, calling themselves "chiefs of Hades." They are smeared
with white clay and dressed up very fantastic-
ally, and, as they can turn themselves into lions
and other wild beasts the better to avenge their
fancied wrongs and dislikes, every one holds

them in great fear. Furthermore, the Manganja
of Nyassaland believe that Mulungu's people are
the spirits, and that He arranges them in rows
or tiers. The Yaos compare the universe to a
house of three storeys. The higher region of
the sky is occupied by Mulungu, the sun and
moon. The second storey is the present abode
of men who came originally from the upper,
and when a man dies he is said to be summoned
by those who are in Hades beneath, where he
joins the great majority in the lower storey.

Bantu negroes have lost their old conceptions
of heaven, although they are not forgotten in
the folktales. The Wagogo have a legend
about the *Origin of Fire* which illustrates the
point. Long ago there was no fire on the
earth, and so a man went up to look for it in
the sky. In the first heaven he came across
a number of men who seemed to have lost
their better halves. At least they had all but
one side a-piece, and at the sight the man
laughed heartily. In the second heaven he
found people walking on their heads, and again
laughed at them. In the third heaven he met
people crawling on their hands and knees, and
again laughed them to scorn. When he asked
them the way, they told him to keep right on
until he came to Mulungu's abode, which he
found to be in the fourth heaven.

The sight everywhere was ravishing in the

extreme. Mulungu invited the traveller into a room, and showed him a number of beautiful pots, besides two inferior ones which contained the firebrand he wanted. When asked to take his choice, the man selected one of the beautiful pots and brought it to earth, where he found it contained nothing but charcoal. Thus was he punished for despising God's children. A second and third man went up and came down with the like result. At last a woman was persuaded to ascend. She sang to the deformed children of Mulungu, and they were greatly taken with her, and advised her what to do. On she wandered till she reached Mulungu's abode, when she chose the inferior pot and came to earth with it. In this manner the world was supplied with fire; and in their better moods men say that women are more sensible than they.

Another common type of tale may be instanced from the *Story of the Wicked Sisters.* The youngest sister, deluded by her elders, flung her baby-boy into a river; and not till she saw her only child devoured by a crocodile would she believe the treachery of her sisters. She thereupon appealed to Mulungu, and made her way to his realm by climbing a tree. This tree, like that of Jack the Giant-Killer, reached far into heaven; and by its means she passed through the realms of beasts, birds, and fishes. As she showed a warm heart towards the dumb creation, the

beasts readily pointed out the way to Mulungu's
abode, and gave her their blessing.   Soon after
she entered God's village, who heard her plaint,
and made the crocodile restore the child.   Then
the sisters, jealous of the other's good fortune,
threw their babies into the river and climbed up
the tree.   As they went, they reviled the beasts,
birds, and fishes; and Mulungu, seeing them to
be false, gave them a bottle of his lightning and
said, "Your children are in here."   The bottle
burst with a loud crash, and killed the false sisters
instantly.   Such was the divine punishment for
facing God with a lie.

It may not be irrelevant to note in passing
that the negro superstition of climbing a wonderful tree to reach God's abode is known to
European lore.   The shaman-doctor of Russia
cuts nine steps on the sacred birch-tree, by which
means he rises to the sky.   He traverses various
zones of heaven till he reaches the highest, and
communes with *Yayuchi*, the Creator.[1]

In the old folklore of Europe, a belief in the
Many Mansions was very popular.   The Greeks
idealised, among other ethereal places, the abodes
of Tartarus, Erebus, and the White Isle, which
was reserved for the bravest heroes, like the two
Ajaces.   The Elysian Fields were for the most
select, and above all else.   They have been
located in the Fortunate Isles off the African

[1] *Journ. Anthrop. Inst.*, vol. xxi. p. 77.

Coast in the Atlantic; and by other classical
writers were supposed to be in the isle of Peuce.
Virgil said they were in Italy; Lucian put them
near the moon; while Plutarch thought them
near the centre of the earth. Elysium was, however, a state of spiritual being, and, naturally
enough, had no geographical position on earth.

The Nine Celestial Worlds.—In the
Norse Eddas, Scandinavian mythology represents the ash-tree *Yggdrasil* as standing in the
well of the Urdar fountain, with its branches
towering up through the nine worlds to the
highest heaven. This plurality of mansions is
looked after by *Hela*, goddess of the Underworld,
who is said to "have the government of nine
distinct worlds into which she sends and dis-
tributes those who are sent to her"; and
Heimdall's trumpet could be heard throughout
all these worlds.[1] According to tradition, these
nine worlds included (1) *Muspellheim*, which lay
farthest south and was considered the highest
heaven with light, warmth, and fire, and older
than heaven and earth; (2) *Asgard* or *Godheim*,
the home of the gods; (3) *Vanaheim*; (4) *Mid-
gard* or *Manheim*; (5) *Alfheim*, the place of the
elves; (6) *Svart Alfheim*; (7) *Jotunheim* or
Utgard, where the wonderful giants lived;
(8) *Helheim*, the world of spectres; and (9)
Niflheim, the world of mist, uninhabited and

[1] Mallet's *Northern Antiquities*, pp. 95, 96.

lying farthest north. Such were the nine celestial worlds of the ancient Scandinavians, the
conception of which they had probably borrowed
from an older heathen creed.

The nine ranks of the nine worlds have been
already illustrated in Celtic folklore, and it remains to specify the latter belief. The celestial
countries of which the poets mostly sing are
Mag Mell, the Plain of Happiness; *Tir Tairn-
gaire*, the Land of Promise; *Tir nan Og*, the
Land of the Ever-Young; and *Tir fo Thuinn*,
Land Underwaves. Other places mentioned are
the *Big Island of the Spirit of the Mist*; *Beautiful Isle of the Shadow of the Stars*; *Isle of the
Giants*, where the three bottles of magic balsam
(*tri ballan iochshlaint*) are kept; and the *Uttermost World*, where are the trees with the golden
apples. Perhaps the old belief is best seen in
the tale of *Fionn 'an tigh a' Bhlàir Bhuidhe*.
Of Fionn, an old deity of the heathen Britons, it
is said that his whistle could pass through the
seven borders of the worlds, and to the extremity
of the *Uttermost World*.[1] And as beyond the
Uttermost World lay the Green Isle or Land
Underwaves, we have the full complement of
the nine worlds,—analogous in a Slav tale to
the nine kingdoms through which the hero
Niezguniak searches for his bride. He finds her

---

[1] 'Nuair a sheinneadh e i, rachadh a fuaim roimh sheachd
iomaill an domhain agus gu iomall an Domhain Toir.

at last by means of his magic horse, which, like the Gaelic Pegasus, is as ready on sea as on land.

Over the whole negro area it will be manifest from the above evidence how the ancients knew that the Unseen was divided into several mansions, which accorded with the rank of spirits, all of whom obtained place by virtue of their spiritual worth and dignity. When Christ came into the world, He taught anew a doctrine which had been revealed to man ages before; but with this difference, that faith in Him, and obedience to His commandments, came before a mere knowledge of the occult.

Negro Conceptions of Heaven.—In the ancient philosophy of the Druid priests of Britain, the soul was held to be immortal, and not subject to the power of death. Death was indeed the key which opened the door to Eternity. Lucan, writing about 65 A.D., thus apostrophises the British Druids : "And ye, ye Druids, now that the sword was removed, began once more your barbaric rites and weird solemnities. To you only is given knowledge and ignorance (whichever it be) of the gods and the powers of heaven. Your dwelling is in the lone heart of the forest; from you we learn that the bourne of man's ghost is not the senseless grave nor the pale realm of the monarch below ; in another world his spirit survives still. Death, if your lore be true, is but the passage to enduring life." The Druids, as an institution in the land, and the religious precepts they taught, long survived the Roman attempts at suppression. Their ideas of the other world are shown very clearly in old Celtic literature, for the Druid of one age became the Christianised monk of the next.

An old fairy-tale, narrating the exploits of the divine Fionn, remarks that "it was not fit for one to enter a fairy-knoll or *síde* with a blemish." It was sin, because it was the mark of impurity. Another and more celebrated fairy-tale, known as *Tochmarc Etaine*, expresses in very beautiful language how death is the passage to a land of delight. It reflects, however, the spirit of the age, for its joys are of the earth earthy rather than spiritual. The fairy-lady from the land of the immortals sings thus in flowing strain: "Wonderful is the land, the land of which I speak, where youth attains not age; a land where warm sweet streams meander through, flowing with the choicest of mead and wine. Handsome are the men of unblemished form bearing no sin nor guile; and although we survey all around, yet are we seen of none."[1]

The beautiful land of the immortals, appointed for those without sin or blemish, is not forgotten by the Basques of to-day. The place of *Etaine* is taken by *Maitagarri*, a lovely fairy who lives

[1] *Irish Texts*, vol. i. p. 133.

in the mountain-lakes, and has a palace made all of crystal. Like Etaine or the Congo Queen of the Fairies, she fell in love with a mortal, and wanted to marry a shepherd, *Luzaide* by name, whom she took to the summit of *Ahunemendi*, where was her palace. Another time she wooed a virtuous youth, Juan de Arpide by name, who was proof against her charms. She lays forth to him the glories of her celestial country: " Listen to me," she says to Juan, "and I will make you the happiest of mortals. Do you wish for glory? Speak, and the crown of the conqueror will encircle your brow. Do you wish for wealth? Ask, and you shall see palaces rising up to receive you; brilliant shields to defend you; costly robes to adorn you; maidens and pages to serve you. Do you yearn for love? You will possess mine eternally—a love which cannot be compared with any other."[1] To such a tale as this, the Irish folktale bears striking resemblance, and the latter, for more reasons than one, would obviously seem to have been handed down from the Basques of Britain to the Celtic peoples who displaced them.

The Zulus have several tales about the kingdom of heaven, but two will suffice to illustrate. According to one tradition, a man paid a visit to the bourne of spectres, being conducted there by a large lion which put him into a great cavern where the ancestors dwelt.

[1] Monteiro's *Basque Legends*, p. 111.

The road was long and narrow, and the spirits did not like to have a human being among them ; so they gave him what he wanted and sent him back again to earth. When he returned, he told his friends that the spirits lived very happily together, and had plenty cattle. But everyone was small in stature, and the houses and cattle were small in proportion. Such was the condition of the "mitey" dead.

The happiness of the sanctified spirits is attested by the *Tale of the Resurrected Brother* who visited his old home. He said that he had been in a fine country ; that the corn and sugar-cane grew thick and tall, and the cattle were as fat as fat could be. The Wagogo legend of the *Origin of Fire* in a similar way affirms how ravishing is the sight of God's village. Taken in conjunct with the other legends it shows that the kingdom of *i-zulu* is a closer reality to the negro than to the civilised or cultured mind.

The Land of Beulah.—Among a few negro tribes a technical name is given to heaven— the Land of *Beulah*, the Abode of the Blest. In West Africa, where the old Papuan race still flourishes, the word is only used in this sense ; and, according to Dr. Deniker, prevails among the Dualas of the Cameroons. The custom of holding the Feast of the Dead for nine days is observed amongst them, and the nine-day period is supposed to be the time that the

soul takes on its journey to *Bela*, the place of
eternal rest.[1] With the Kaffir-Zulus, it appears
as *Mbulu* or Styx, to the demons of which the
magicians sometimes pray.

The history of the word goes back to the
remote period when the Bengal negroes learned
it from the Papuans, and possibly also the ideas
connected therewith. The Malanaus of North
Borneo believe in another world which is like
this, having rivers, seas, mountains, and sago
plantations. The supreme deity is *Ipu* or Jahweh,
and to him there corresponds a beautiful female
spirit, *Balu Adad*, who conducts departed souls to
their future abode. The narrow road leading to
Beulah is guarded by the double-headed dog
Mawiang, and he is a good ghost that gets a free
pass without a bite. In Melanesia, Hades is called
Bulaiva, and in Fiji, *Mbulu*.[2] The latter people
excuse their practice of widow-strangling by
saying that necessity compels them. On the
road to Mbulu, a terrible god, by name *Nangga-
nangga*, lies in wait, and is most implacable
towards unmarried men and those who have not
brought their wives with them. Therefore the
rule is that at least one wife should accompany
her husband in death ; and this was, till lately,
observed in India under the form of the suttee.

Beulah is not without a history, for everywhere

[1] *The Races of Man*, p. 243.
[2] *Journ. Anthrop. Inst.*, vol. x. p. 139.

it is made synonymous with heaven. But it is a far country reached with difficulty. The Cerberus of the Papuan tales becomes the lion of the Zulu tales, and the sacrifice of wives and beasts is hoped to lessen the toils of the journey. Even this may not be enough to soothe Cerberus if he feels that the earthly record of the soul is unclean. Perhaps a man breaks his country's tabus and customs; he commits sin, and the sinful cannot pass Cerberus unscathed by his iron teeth. The conception that underlies all this class of folklore is that sin cannot enter the kingdom of God, the New Jerusalem of Beulah.

The Death-Journey. — It is not readily apparent what made the ancients believe that death brought with it trials and tribulations to good and bad alike. The latter suffered more acutely from the ills of earth without becoming morally quickened; the former were relieved from these, but still had to go a long and wearisome journey ere they reached the "Land o' the Leal." The deceased, however, whether good or bad, was supplied with food, clothing, and arms, so that he might suffer as little inconvenience as possible from hunger, cold, or peril on the voyage. In Zulu, the expression "He has gone on a long journey" is more than a stock phrase. By it is conveyed to the negro mind the toils of the journey that the dead begins with his new life. And the Zulus are not alone in believing that death will bring spiritual troubles which the living can partly relieve.

Asceticism, in India, is a common way of lessening the troubles after death, and from that it is but a step to add loads of religious duties and penances. The Maiwar Bhils of Rajputana go much further in their sacrifices. "Heaven is supposed to be but a short distance from earth, but the souls of the dead have to reach it by a very painful and weary journey, which can be avoided to some extent during life by ascending high hills and there depositing images of the horse, which, in addition to reminding the gods of the work already accomplished, shall serve as chargers upon which the soul may ride a stage to bliss." [1]

The Kol negroes have possibly derived their idea of Charon's boat, which waits on the dead, from a strange custom they have relating to burial. The Santals believe that the spirits go to *Huripuri*, where they enjoy hunting and ploughing their fields, free from the attentions of the Hindu money-lender, and spend a happy life eating, drinking, and hunting for ever and ever. They will have fine houses wherein to dwell, and nothing will mar the pleasure of their social gatherings. But before all this can come to pass, the body of the deceased must be thrown into the sacred stream, whether it be the Damuda or

---

[1] *Journ. Beng. Asiat. Soc.*, vol. xliv. p. 348.

Ganges. After cremation, the pieces of bone (*jang baha*) are rescued from the pyre and consigned, with much ceremony, to the river. Then the *Bhandan* ceremonies are observed after returning from the place where the bones were deposited.

Were these rites and ceremonies neglected, the disembodied spirit would not fare well on the death-journey. Neither would it be allowed to associate with those who had gone before. Being a recognised outcast on earth, it would remain so after death, and would be separated from the ancestors in some humbler spiritual abode, ruled over, perhaps, by an archdemon. The names of the nine rulers of the dead are not made clear in Santal traditions, and only four can be given for certain—*Jom Hudar, Jom Raja, Hudul Raja,* and *Singbonga.*

The Ship of the Dead.—Burial at sea and the purifying of the dead form part of the Santal's ritual to get the soul through Purgatory. Nevertheless, the former custom is more characteristic of the Papuans of the Indian Archipelago than of any Indian people. Among them the bodies of the poor were usually flung into the sea to hasten their journey, while the rich were set adrift in boats, the corpses being richly apparelled. The custom was dropped in quite recent times through the natives discovering their neighbouring enemies tricked out in the finery of their deceased relatives. Since then the Boats of the Dead no longer hasten the departed on their way.

In other regions, Charon's boat becomes mythical and less matter-of-fact. Ghosts are said in Florida Isle to assemble in the west till a magic canoe takes them over to the other world. When they have crossed the river of death they first realise that they are dead, and then they go through numerous adventures which it would be here irrelevant to discuss. Fijian ghosts have Jumping-off Places, *thombo-thombo*, which are usually steep cliffs facing the regions whence, says tradition, the Papuans originally came.[1] Then they are ferried over to the land of shadows to start on the long road without the proverbial turning, the Path of the Dead (*Salo ni Yalo*).

It is typical of Papuan faith in the South Sea Islands that, when a man is about to die, he sees a canoe manned by some of his predeceased friends, who come with the tide to bid him welcome to their celestial country. "Come with us," they say, "come into the land of light; come into the land of great things, wonderful things; come into the land of plenty where hunger is unknown; come with us and rest for evermore. The birds of our country will bring you delicious berries; the dogs of our city will furnish you with

[1] *Journ. Anthrop. Inst.*, vol. xxiv. p. 349.

innumerable bear-skins ; and your home will be made of beautiful cedar, all inset with most lovely shells. Come with us into our land of sunshine, and be a great chief, attended with numerous slaves. Come with us now, for the tide is about to ebb and we must depart."

The lore surrounding Charon's boat and the long sea-journey before the soul has gone through the waters of death is found among other peoples. An echo of this is seen in the Zulu idiom, *ulwandhle luvile*, "the sea is dead"—a poetic phrase for the ebbing of the tide. And with this, again, may be compared a superstition in West Wales that souls do not leave the earth till ebbtide.

Speeding the Departed.—To lessen the toils of ghostly wayfarers it is customary to make sacrifices on the dead's behoof. A very popular kind of sacrifice, especially among the wealthy, was the slaughter of a horse on which the spirit might ride ; while poorer people contented themselves with less expensive offerings. Natives of Central India believe that by holding on to the tail of a calf a dying man will be considerably helped over the River of Death. The Bhils of Rajputana make images of horses for the dead to ride on ; and the custom seems to be a survival from an older age when horses were sacrificed to the dead.

The horse thus becomes intimately associated

with the gods, human and divine. The natives
of Malabar worship the goddess *Yerenamma*, who
is always seen riding a white horse with a sword
in her right hand. Her chief duty is to protect
fishermen from drowning, and from being caught
by big fish. The goddess *Bhagadevi*, however,
rides a tiger and protects the community from
cholera. Of other deities, some ride elephants;
but as a rule the horse is more popular, as
elephants are never considered suitable animals
for sacrifice to the gods.

Among the Kols the horse no longer plays
any part in funeral ceremonies, and yet tradition
makes much of the horses of the olden time.
One of these is named *Sing Sadom*, "day-horse,"
a creature which appears in many tales and
legends of the Santals, especially those dealing
with the Creation.

Nor do the Bantu attach much importance to
the horse or zebra, their place being taken by
animals which appeal more to the curious minds
of the natives. The otter, *umtini*, is said to
have horns, and dwells in the pools where the
rainbow enters; while other animals have their
habits duly chronicled. But among the Suahili
the old belief in a death-sacrifice crops out in the
symbolical fashion, as in India. A particular
kind of hare, named *Kipanawazi*, is believed to
ferry men over a river after death; and it
would be difficult to dissociate this superstition

from the more ancient custom of sacrificing horses.

Outside the negro area the lore about the horse seems to be much the same. Among the Lapps the snake *Saiva Guelle* usurps its place. When a man is sick the priest has to seek the soul in the other worlds, and rides on the back of this snake to *Yabme Aimo*, the Land of Shadows. There he has sometimes to wrestle with the wicked spirits before he can restore the sick man's soul to earth. The shamans of the Altaians, when sacrificing to the supreme God, choose a suitable horse, whose soul they expel by means of incantations and charms. This is their offering to the deity. Among the Buryats the shaman-doctor takes great pride in his tambourine. It is his fetish, and to him its chief importance is that it represents the horse which can carry him whithersoever he will. The tambourine with the Yakut shamans is venerated for a like reason, and is further adorned with rattles and bells.

When a shaman dies the corpse is borne to the grave on a gaily-caparisoned steed, one old man sitting behind the corpse to balance it, and another old man to lead. The nine sons or companions of the shaman meanwhile keep up a mournful dirge, while the old men and brother shamans ring bells and beat the tambourines. At the grave the horse is sacrificed, and the mourners depart, never daring to look back for fear the deceased shaman might carry them off to the sky.

From the foregoing examples it is therefore historically certain that the ancient negroes thought that at death the spirit had a long and toilsome way to go, and that the sacrifice of animals on which the spirit might ride alleviated the weariness of the journey. By the same means doctors were enabled to search for the wandering souls of their sick patients, but in both cases the horse was supposed to have a spirit, and for the time being acted the part of a subconscious medium. During the spirit-journey no mortal wight dared venture off his steed. To fall or step off the spiritual Pegasus brought instant death.

The Nine Rivers of Death.—The spiritual significance conveyed in the number nine has been already instanced among the Bantu, as in the Duala Nine Days' Feast of the Dead, and the nine attendants in Congoland on the Queen of the Fairies. Through its spiritual associations nine becomes a sacred number, and soon attaches itself to the native ritual. It then assumes the formality of sacerdotalism, shrouded in symbolism and mystery.

In Uganda nine is the sacred number. When a priest begins his cure he selects nine articles, eight of which are plain, while the ninth is stitched with cowrie shells. The doctor's fee is nine cowrie shells for assurance money, but a further fee is paid whenever his patient is cured. Should twins be born in a house the father takes nine cowrie shells and a seed of the wild banana to the priest. On seeing them the priest divines the father's mission from the quaint symbol; while with the Wagogo nine knots tied on a string symbolise a wife's pregnancy.

The people of Loanda look on the number with peculiar regard. With them it is the mark of superlative excellence, so that when one form of excellence is surpassed by another, and the people cannot tell which is best, they will say that one is the ninth but the other is the tenth. Beauty would be described thus: *O manii a, se uauaba kavua, o mona uauaba kakuinii;* "if her mother was beautiful the ninth, the daughter was beautiful the tenth." Such sort of native idiom is clearly dependent on the old Bantu ritual, which held nine to be sacred because it was the symbol of spiritual perfection.

Although it is an irrelevance in this work to discuss beliefs among peoples who claim no affinity by blood and language with the Kol and Bantu negroes, exception may be made in a few undernoted cases.

To the ancient Aztecs of Mexico the belief in the Many Mansions was familiar. They admitted a series of gradations in the happiness prepared for men. Warriors who foremost fighting fell went straight to the House of the Sun. But for obscurer people and lieges—like those who fought and bled for king and country at Bannock-burn — were found less brilliant homes in the various stars peopling the firmament. When a plebeian died, a stone called *tentell* was put between his lips, and this obol, along with other offerings and liturgical formulas, served the deceased's passport to the other world.

If the dead man had been a chief, noble, or wealthy landowner, the death-ceremonies were more elaborate. At the funeral a little red-haired dog was killed, and, with a leash of cotton tied round its neck, was buried beside its master. This sacrifice of the faithful hound, in public opinion, made sure that the dog's spirit would perform the important duty of helping his master's soul across the *chicunahuapan*, or " Nine Torrents."

Nadaillac sees in the rivers of death a mere allusion to the nine Mexican firmaments where souls had to sojourn during their successive migrations ; but in this he was greatly mistaken. For example, in the various religions of China to-day, the belief in the nine heavens is no longer maintained, although it seems to have formerly existed. The state in China contains nine degrees of ranks, each of which has a separate emblem of honour taken from a particular animal. The country itself was supposed to have been

divided into nine parts during the rule of the
legendary king Yu, who also mapped out the
nine divisions of the heavens on a generous
scale; and the sacred cap of the Emperor is
distinguished by nine seams which only the
Son of Heaven may vaunt. From all this it is
easy to see and understand that in Mexico and
China the number nine was sacred because of
its spiritual associations. There were anciently
believed to be nine heavenly mansions and nine
rivers of death.

The latter belief is more intelligible to the
average Chinaman. Tradition says that when a
person dies his soul departs to the netherworld,
and is there prevented from recrossing to enjoy
earthly scenes by nine torrents. *Kew sing chow
shan*, they say, which means, according to Dr.
Morrison's translation, "Nine circling streams
the captive souls enclose." In addition, the
connection of the Pierian Well with the dead
is clearly set forth in the superstition of *Kew
Tseuen*, "Nine watersprings;" and it is of this
well that the Chinese speak when they refer to
the departed spirits as being there, knowing what
is done on earth but unable to cross the waters of
death.

Among the Lapps and the Finns, *Tuoni* is
the god of death, and another name for him is
Mana or *Manalainen*. Those who took the
long journey to *Tuonela* or *Manala* had to cross

nine seas and a river which was as inky-black as the Styx, deep and violent, and full of hungry whirlpools and angry waterfalls. The soul's happiness was perfected when the last of the nine seas was safely crossed, the last bourne gained—

> " When appear Tuoni's islands
> And the hilltops of Manala."

The servants of the gods of the Rivers of Death are the kelpies and water-sprites of folk-lore. In Highland lore, the sight of a *baobh* or water-spirit washing clothes is reckoned a sure portent that some member of the community will shortly be drowned. The water-sprite is sup-planted in the *Kalevala* by the daughter of the god of death, and her washing the clothes in the rivers of death similarly portends death to mortals. "The dwarfish daughter of Tuoni, the stunted maiden of Manala, was seen wash-ing dirty linen, beating clothes in the black river of Tuoni, in the marsh-water of Manala."

The Death-Waters of Druidic Tradi-tion.—But if evidence among the Bantu about the Nine Rivers of Death is to-day meagre and unsatisfactory, it is less so in Great Britain where it is more plentiful. Old and modern Celtic literature both teach how popular were the spiritual messages of the Druids ; and this in turn proves the great interdependence of Basque and Celt in the early annals of our country.

Concomitant with the Druidic belief in the nine spiritual worlds was that of the nine seas or torrents which every soul had to traverse ere the abode of bliss was attained. The Great Spirit dwelling in the Highest, the House of the Sun, ruled over nine worlds. In his kingdom of the universe were many worlds wherein to accommodate the living dead according to their works; but the Elect, the highest of the nine grades, were alone suffered to approach the majesty of God and be for ever with the Lord. Thus while the fortunate Elect might have a length of happy days, the bad and indifferent, classed as the damned on the downgrade, would be apportioned in one or other of the lower mansions affording special facilities for ruminating and groaning and gnashing of teeth. Their sorrows unheard could not cross the ninth of the lethal waters.

A fair idea of this is conveyed in a mediæval Irish text. The dying saint has far to travel after death; but once his soul has reached the sun and there entered the presence of the Great Unknown, he is beyond the pang of sorrow and misfortune: "With the life of his soul in the realm of the White Sun, borne past miseries in the hills of the seven heavens"—

> "La bethaid a anmae
> Hi flaith Greni Gile
> Iarna breith sechingra
> Fordingna secht nime."

A poem of the tenth century on the *Day of Judgment* addresses God with the strange title of King of the Sun (*Rí Grene*),—apparently after the old manner of the Druids. But in the homily of the "Evernew Tongue" (*Tenga Bithnua*), God is styled the "King of the Seven Heavens," in the second zone of which are nine fiery pillars to the south supporting it. Although the older belief pertaining to the nine torrents seems obscured by passages as these, it reveals itself very frequently elsewhere, thus showing how the old monks, presumably of Celtic blood and education, mixed up Druidic doctrine and belief with the tenets of Christianity.

The soul must cross the nine torrents to reach the abode of bliss. The ninth torrent or wave, therefore, procures happiness and cures ills. For instance, in the *Tripartite Life of St. Patrick*, it is said that pestilence never comes over nine waves—

"Ni thic teidm dar nói tonna."

And in the *Tale of the Ordeals*, a story is told of Morann, son of Cairbre Cat-head, who lived in the first century of our era. Morann was born with a malformation, but was cured of it by virtue of the healing powers in the ninth wave. The supernatural element in the story is introduced by a man from the fairymounds, who advised Morann's mother what to do with the child. Likewise in Wales the number nine appears to have been synonymous with perfection and happiness; and thus the city built on the ninth wave is the New Jerusalem set on a tideless sea—*Adwyn gaer yssyd ar ton nawvet.*

The Gaels of Scotland were in nowise behind their Irish brethren in maintaining kindred beliefs. Early writers called them godless pagans and naked heathen; the modern say they were pious and emotional. In the words of a Scotch Gaelic professor who has well eulogised them from a feeling of mutual admiration: "The Celts have always had the reputation of being a religious people, and nowhere would we fain believe has Christianity found more faithful and devoted disciples than among the Celts of those Isles. It may well be that the aspect of religion which especially attracts the Celts is that which appeals to the feelings rather than to the understanding. The language is wonderfully copious in its vocabulary of adoration and praise." And if all cuss-words and pointed execrations of the Saxon be excluded from Gaelic, the piety of the Highland Host and other "Hielant Teevils" goes without saying.

That among the Gaels the number nine was devoted peculiarly to the realm of the supernatural is everywhere made evident. For instance, in an unpublished Gaelic tale, a man, we are told, was enabled to arouse the Fenian warriors by a whistle obtained from the oldest of nine old men, fathers and sons. This magic whistle could be heard throughout the nine worlds. In another tale, Fionn is said to have learned swimming from Luas Lurgan, the sister of Cumall. Very soon he could swim better than his tutor, so that he could swim over the nine waves and be ashore before her. To produce the need-fire or purificatory *teine-eigin* from an oak log by rapidly boring with an auger, was a task allotted to the nine nines of first-begotten sons—*naoi naoinear ceud ginealaich mac.*

The *Bodhar Bacach* of tradition could not hear the latest joke till nine nines shouted it in his ear; and it was then no joke as he was as deaf as a post. The berries of a certain rowan-tree in Loch Mai, says the *Book of the Dean of Lismore*, could suffice for a man's nine meals. They could also add a year to his life. Of a later age was Duncan Ban's prescription for a love-charm. Nine ferns should be cut with an axe, and three bones of an old man taken from a grave. They were next to be burnt to ashes, and the ashes thrown against the north wind. This magic spell overcomes the pensive scruples of any wilful maid, who marries the enchanter on the spot and tries to live happily together ever after.

But illustrative of the main point regarding the curative powers of the ninth wave or torrent, an example may be culled from the Middle Irish compilation known as *Acallamh na Senorach*, otherwise, if freely rendered, "Old Men's Palavers." The hero Caoilte once felt sick and ill at ease; and, distrusting the local practitioners who took large fees for experimenting on people in the cause of science, he sought supernatural advice from a fairy-lady and got it gratis—of first importance to Caoilte. This Queen of the Fairies, *Bebhionn* by name, brought magic herbs in a basin from Fairyland, and by their means was Caoilte cured. In Gaelic lore, the same kind of cure is applied, but the herbs of magic are sought for beyond the nine seas of death, and the benevolent fairy is supplanted by the Virgin Mary, who crosses them on behalf of those who seek her spiritual aid—

"Chaidh Muire thar na naoi maranan
A bhuain na torranain."

The other power derived from the supernatural was that of crossing the nine rivers. When Fergus, the Irishman, asked the fairy for power to walk under seas, lochs, and pools, the fairy granted permission, except in the case of Loch Rudhraidhe, which was in his own country. Then the fairies put magic herbs in his ears, and he went under the seas in their company. According to other traditions, he was given a magic hood, which rendered the wearer invisible and enabled him to walk along the bottom of the sea. Another legend says that the fairies haunt the wells of Ireland, and are often to be seen appearing above the surface and speaking to men.

Sometimes the fairy's girdle plays the leading rôle. In the folktale of the Rape of Proserpine, Ceres discovers the whereabouts of her daughter by finding her girdle floating on the surface of Cyane, the "well," near which Pluto had descended into the netherworld with his earthly bride. The Zulu tale of *The Princess and the Imbulu* (lizard) also brings the magic girdle into prominence, for by it the lizard was enabled to assume her shape and princely bearing. The folklore of Scottish Gaelic has a similar love for connecting the magic girdle with the fairies and the nine seas of death. One couplet, first of all, connects the nine gods or fairies, the Nine Maidens, with the nine roads or paths of the dead—

> "Naoi conair 'us naoi conachair,
> 'Us naoi bean-seanga sith."

Another story is still more explanatory, and relates the sorrows of a poor man inconsolable for the loss of his better half, tongue-tied for ever. Earthly means proved unavailing to restore her to life, and his last resource was to seek superhuman aid. Accordingly he approached the fairies to help him, and one more compassionate than the rest gave him her fairy girdle. "This," she said, "will bring her back from the lands of the dead, even though the nine deaths were in her mouth "—

"Ged a bhiodh na naoi bais 'na beul."

Socrates on the Many Mansions.—With such beliefs among the heathen races of Britain may be profitably compared those once current in Pelasgian Greece, for the Nine Rivers are not without mention in the old literature of Greece. The celebrated Pierian Well was connected with Apollo and the Nine Muses—

"The sisters of the sacred well
That from beneath the seat of Jove doth spring."

They were symbolically set over its nine springs, but in reality were bound up with the worship of the dead. This is made clearer from customs in other lands. In England, for instance, many circles of the great Standing-Stones go by the name of the *Nine Maidens*, — perhaps named from their hardness of heart.

In Arcadia, the country of an ancient negro race, the Styx was venerated because of its sacredness; and oaths by it became inviolable, no matter what it might cost a Phaethon or Semele. As its waters disappeared into the earth a little below the fountainhead, it was accounted a river of hell; but while such was the local tradition, there prevailed an older and genuine belief which said that the Styx flowed nine times round hell. Hades was therefore a place of many mansions.

The Greek idea of Hades governed by its king *Hudul Raj* was of Pelasgian origin, and along with the rivers of Hades formed an outstanding feature of Pelasgian belief. The Socratic view of these rivers was doubtless the common opinion of the day, and Socrates justified it by argument. The soul had to undertake a long journey after death, because there were many rivers to cross and barriers to negotiate. If there were not, what need of so many δαιμωνες to conduct the souls of men? Were there not branches and tortuous windings of the Rivers of Death, none could miss the way. And again, what need had the dead of elaborate rites and sacrifices unless the Paths of the Dead were full of snares and unknown dangers? The dreaded Powers of the Unseen were no shadowy spectres, but mighty forces before whom the bravest dead might quail.

It would appear from all this that the old Pelasgians feared the journey to the after-life more than death itself, or else why did the living try to help the dead on their way by chanting prayers, requiems, and masses, and offering sacrifices to appease the Powers of the Unseen? Such needless cares were undoubtedly meant for good, but all are alike in displaying an indescribable fear of what the after-life brought to sinful man. His harshest judge was his load of guilt and sin, and the heavier it was

13